THE CRANBROOK CHRONICLES

Deborah VanderJagt
a.k.a. Debbie Dailey

Cover Design by Andrew Marquez

ISBN: 978-1-5356-0631-8

Contents

Preface

As I DRIVE DOWN THE narrow suburban street called Cranbrook Road, creeping as slowly as I can without the inhabitants of the little houses thinking I am some sort of a weird stalker, the homes look smaller than my memory recalls, the vegetation seems overgrown, and there is a lack of children darting back and forth across the street. Now, I see it—my childhood bedroom window.

I remember standing on my bed and staring out of it to see if I could get a glimpse of the Knight boys across the street. Thoughts of childhood crushes, the noise of kids yelling and playing, memories of the busy, bustling neighborhood it was fifty years ago—all rush into my brain.

If I could only, even for just one hour, go back in time to relive the energy and innocence we had during those years. Growing up in an era of economic boom, we, the babies of that boom, inherently were handed a *time in place* that we took advantage of to the max.

Each of us has our own story of growing up, and everyone's story is different. As children, we begin our journey with a fresh canvas, new acrylics, and time on our side. We look through unfiltered eyes at the mysterious world before us as a place of discovery and learning. In our souls we know there is much to be absorbed and figured out before we are eventually handed the responsibility of adulthood.

The challenges we experience as children mold us and shape us. Our perceptions will be designed and will most likely be jaded.

All of the curves and turns, the people who have come in and out of our lives, the choices we make along the way, and what life hands us, all of this will form the beings that we become. What would have happened if I had just...? Why didn't I...?

The following pages are my interpretations of my life as a child. These are the memories that play in my mind, a video of my soul, and my vision of how I remember living in the mid-twentieth century. I hope you enjoy reliving a bit of it with me.

Chapter 1
Welcome to the Neighborhood

"Little boxes all the same; there's a green one and
a pink one and a blue one and a yellow one. And
they're all made out of ticky tacky and they all look
just the same."
—Sung by *Pete Seeger, 1963*

MY EARLY-LEARNING DAYS WERE LIVED on Cranbrook Road—
and the adjoining streets, all seemingly named after liberal arts
colleges and galleries—Chesterfield, Hampshire, Radcliffe, and
Towner—in Ann Arbor, Michigan. That was back when the
summers seemed longer than winters, the map of my life was
just beginning to be charted, and adventure seemed just a step
away, at the edge of the lawn.

The "cracker box" houses in our subdivision, named Kensington Farms, all had the exact same one-thousand-square-foot floor plan except for the one optional wall between the living and dining rooms. You could choose the "open" concept or the "closed off, very small dining room" concept. Either way, they were brand-new and "state of the art" in 1956, the year my family moved in.

Even though all of the floor plans were exactly alike, the exteriors were different. Well, at least four different styles to choose from. The builders would not put any of the same styles next to each other, so there was, of course, some integrity to the project. Because it had a porch that ran along one half of the front, with square pillars framing the large, energy-inefficient "picture" window, I liked our house the best. No garages—they were considered a luxury, not a necessity, in the 1950s. Every home was equipped with a built-in milk box next to the back door for the milkman's deliveries. Our mother ordered milk, butter, and cottage cheese on a piece of notepaper she would slip into the box the night before he was scheduled to arrive. A milk box was just a hole through the wall to the outside with a metal door on each side. Quite an invention. Gone were the days of heating with coal; now forced-air natural-gas furnaces were the modern way.

With their affordable three bedrooms and one bath, the houses attracted mostly families who were just starting out. The many young parents in the Kensington Farms subdivision all seemed to be striving for the promise of an illuminating future. The endless possibilities, a chance to have the good life, and the hope that their children would have it better than they did. Mothers stayed home raising the kids and dads were off to work. There were doctors, engineers, entrepreneurs, policemen, construction workers, television salesmen, and college professors—a full spectrum of occupations.

Just as various were the attitudes toward rearing children. Some of my best memories are of the Mikkelsens' household. How the Mikkelsen family lived in this tiny house with the many kids of their own, and the neighborhood kids who invaded it, always amazed me.

Mrs. Mikkelsen enjoyed bearing children; she had six. It was just that she seemed to float through motherhood after the children were past the infant stage. Not that she was totally unaware of what her children were up to; I just don't think she was too concerned about it. Unlike the other mother hens in the neighborhood, Mrs. Mikkelsen didn't worry much about the small stuff. Like eating. Her philosophy was: if the kids are hungry they will come in and find some food. I remember one time, just this once, she was standing in her kitchen one early afternoon slicing a piece of meat for herself from a good-looking rump roast. Seeing a few neighborhood kids in the back doorway, she asked, "Anyone care for a slice?" Usually, we knew, she was fairly oblivious to whether or not the kids ate or drank during the day. So this AMAZED me. Mrs. Mikkelsen was offering us food? I thought I must be dreaming, or something was amiss in the universe! Although a slice of freshly roasted beef tasted mighty fine on a warm summer's day!

At the Mikkelsens', though, you could get away with just about anything. It was fabulous freedom. We spent hours sprawled out on their living room carpet playing Chinese Checkers, Sorry!, or a game of Yahtzee, and wondered if the Ouija board could really predict our future. It told me that I was going to have one child—a boy. And, as you can imagine, later in life, I was a little nervous about my second pregnancy, already having a boy for the first child. But, alas, I have given birth to two fine boys who are quite grown now, disproving the predictions of the mysterious Ouija.

The most fun of all, at the Mikkelsens', was that they had a state-of-the-art stereo system, along with a bookcase of the best album collection known to man. What seemed to be lacking in "normal" nurturing was made up by the finer things in life: music and art. We sang along with Julie Andrews and *The Sound of Music.* Then *West Side Story* and *Bye Bye Birdie* would play over and over. Soundtracks from *Oklahoma!* and *The Music Man* took turns on the turntable as we discussed the strategies of Michigan rummy. We could hoot and holler and run in and out of their house all day long. Juanita, their maid, would just shake her head at us.

Most mothers of the 1950s and '60s weren't overbearing to the point of knowing everything their children were doing at any given moment, but they all talked to each other almost daily, so, you mostly wanted to avoid all moms if possible.

Staying invisible wasn't so hard. To the east we had a glorious creek to explore. The houses on Hampshire Road had "The Creek" at the edge of their backyards, but it was so wooded along

The Creek that no one could see us. Moms would yell, "Don't you be going down to The Creek!" as we flew out the door. But what would summer be if we couldn't get wet?

To the west was a cornfield that separated our Cranbrook subdivision from another neighborhood. Even though the distance was about a block away, the cornfield kept us from communicating with the kids on the other side, and usually, we only socialized with them when we were at school. The cornfield was part of a farm that had sold off property to develop the subdivisions. In the earliest years of living there, a farmer who had sold the land still lived at the farmhouse. My brother Mark, who was one year younger than me, knew him well. The farmer and his wife still had a small-scale farm with a garden and chickens. Mr. Farmer would give Mark tips on growing vegetables and collecting eggs. Once in a while they would allow me to tag along even though I knew I was invading both territory and man-talk. I was never able to break into their manly inner circle, but once the farmer and his wife gave me some fresh-cut rhubarb from the garden next to the barn. Proud and appeased, I was just fine with the consolation prize and took it home to Mom, who cooked it up with some sugar and tapioca.

The world seemed an exciting place to be. As Americans, the momentum of positivity was contagious. We had a mind-set that we could accomplish everything we set out to do. Even in school, our teachers told us that, without a doubt, we could be the president of the United States if we would just put our minds to it.

But, for now, the edge of the lawn was awaiting our growing and usually bare feet. Exploration and adventure meant stubbed toes, skinned knees, and sometimes bruised egos. But when there is a world to face head-on and full force, it's a small price to pay.

Chapter 2
A Time to Every Purpose

"Come mothers and fathers throughout the land
And don't criticize what you don't understand
Your sons and your daughters are beyond your command
Your old road is rapidly agin'
Please get out of the new one if you can't lend a hand
For the times they are a changin'."
—**Sung by** *Bob Dylan, 1963*

NEWS SOURCES, MID-CENTURY, WERE COMPARABLY archaic to the twenty-first century. The local newspaper, *The Ann Arbor News* had a few articles of national news, one column of international news on the right side of the front page, but the rest of it was devoted to local news and gossip. The Ladies

Literary Club was having a tea this Friday. Frank and Lois Jones' daughter, Ann, was recently engaged to John Baker, and Mrs. George Atkins described the dinner party they held down to the Irish lace napkins and white bone china with gold-plated edging. Your birth, your high-school graduation party, your engagement, wedding, military stints, and college graduation were all well documented for inquiring minds to take note.

The 6:00 p.m. and 11:00 p.m. news kept us abreast of anything else we needed to know. There were no conspiracy theories, at least none that we knew about, and the American populace took verbatim, and as fact, the nightly newscast. If Chet Huntley, Walter Cronkite, or David Brinkley reported it, one was not to question. The news even began to scold our parents by saying "It's eleven o'clock; do you know where your children are?"

This decade of the 1950s marked the start of a more carefree life than ever imagined for middle-class America. Most adults, it seemed, were content to accept their fate to work hard, obey the social norms, not to question, and conform to their new modern world. The buzzwords were our "modern conveniences." Washing machines and dryers, refrigerators, faster automobiles, television, frozen foods, pizza, McDonalds, and stereo systems helped families feel more self-sufficient and proud of their accomplishments. Everyone could take care of themselves. Life was good. Life was easy. The future was fabulous! It had to be! We all believed better things were yet to come.

Overall, the expectation of Americans was to believe in, and back up, the United States of America. We knew we were the greatest superpower in the world and Russia was, as we were all told, about as evil as you could get. The United States, on the other hand, was the God-given gift to the entire earth. We were able not only to provide amenities for our own citizens but were able to take care of the poorest of countries with aid and missionaries. As we were taught, at a very young age, the United States would conquer all evil, convert all heathens, and save the world from Communism. We, as a nation, remedied all that ailed the earth, and we did it all with God's blessing. I am really not, in any way, being sarcastic or trying to mitigate, or magnify, what the United States was doing at the time. But as children of the 1950s, and because the generation before us was very proud of their accomplishments in building up their country and the economy, this is what we were led to believe.

Post-World War II parents wanted their children to have a much easier and carefree life than had ever been possible during the Great Depression and The War. Their mission, as they saw it, was to raise children in a world where they saw optimism and endless possibilities for their future. And for the most part it worked. The boomer kids took that thought of having perpetual forward momentum to a degree that their parents did not even pretend to comprehend. It showed up in our adventurous spirits, our experimentation with life, and our questioning of society and even the government. Our parents, I'm sure, wondered where they went wrong.

The only aspect of life I remember *not* questioning was our music. I dove headlong, hook, line, and sinker, into it. The Beatles, and so many artists before and after, formed an era and shaped the minds of the youth: Bob Dylan, The Rolling Stones, Jimi Hendrix, Buffalo Springfield, The Kinks, The Byrds, Led Zeppelin, Cream, The Yardbirds, and Joan Baez. Throw in the whole British Invasion, the synchronized Motown groups, and folk rockers—it was truly the culmination of a "Happening" in the realm of music. The music artists of that time were speaking to the youth in ways that brought understanding and life to us. It was a revolution of culture, and, one after another, original master poets emerged. We soaked it up.

What allowed this generation to feel free enough to put forth music that spoke so fervently to the youth and touched our very souls?

The music station we listened to was CKLW out of Windsor, Canada. Motown was Detroit, and Detroit was Motown, so CKLW played Motown. In between, and right alongside the Motown music, they played other genres. Stevie Wonder was mixed in with the Beatles; Eric Burdon and Otis Redding came right after Simon & Garfunkel. Petula Clark, the 5th Dimension, and Johnny Rivers, played as soon as the Supremes and the Temptations had their play time. Then came the Beach Boys, the Four Tops, the Association, the Miracles, and Gary Lewis & The Playboys. Why, they could all be brothers! It did not matter whether a musical artist was black, white, or any other race—just the music mattered. Music was, in fact, breaking down racial barriers.

Even my grandma "Nonnie" got caught up with it. Naomi was her real name, but her vanity showed. Mom said Nonnie didn't want to be called "Grandma," so *Nonnie* it was. She had always supported and encouraged our childhood notions and the silly phases we went through, so when Beatlemania hit, Nonnie got on board with it. Troll dolls, Barbie dolls, Beatle wigs, Nik-L-Nips, whatever the fad, she was the supplier. Nonnie, all her life, had attempted to keep up with the times, and this new-fangled music was as hip and cool as when she had danced the Charleston.

Beatlemania can be described as a definitive cultural change in music, and also in attitude, for the '60s generation. Young teenage boys went completely bonkers and were quite possessed for a while. They bought Beatle wigs and electric guitars so they could be "chick magnets" because the chicks had fallen in love with John, Paul, George, and Ringo.

The Beatles could do no wrong. Nonnie asked my brother and me what songs we wanted her to put on her Wurlitzer juke box she had next to the bar in her basement. We said, "Any Beatles songs, it doesn't matter which ones, any and all of them are great!" Even though we enjoyed listening to her songs, such as "Big Bad John," Ricky Nelson's "Hello Mary Lou," and some weird song named "Nature Boy," we wanted her to get up to date with some of the tunes.

There were no substitutes either. My parents came home from shopping one night and said, "Look what we bought for you!" They pulled out a record album that said *A Hard Day's Night* on it. My brother looked at it skeptically, not recognizing the album cover that had four heads of Beatle-like hair on it, and below that it said "Featuring the Manchesters." *The Manchesters?* Who were *The Manchesters?* We couldn't believe our parents could be fooled by imposters!

On a Sunday morning in 1965, Grandma Nonnie called our house and said that she had found out from some very mysterious person that the Beatles were coming to Detroit and were staying at the Whittier Hotel. So, she explained, if we stood along the driveway to the entrance of the hotel, we could actually watch the limousine carrying the Fab Four on their way into the hotel. It was beyond Beatle fan belief! A chance to see *them*, the real live Beatles, in person!

Nonnie said I could ask my best friend, Diane, to come along. I knew Diane would absolutely fall over and faint at this opportunity of a lifetime. But, alas, her mom said, "No way." I was completely shocked! Mrs. Knight actually said no to Diane's only chance in life to see THE BEATLES—but it was a Sunday and my grandma Nonnie's reputation preceded her as an "out of the box," well, let's say, wacky, grandmother.

My brother Mark and I did get to go to Detroit. The Whittier Hotel had a long drive up to its entrance, and we marked our territory on the curb and sat down in exhilarating anticipation.

I looked down at my white Keds tennis shoes and came up with a novel idea. I unlaced one of my shoes, thinking that when the limo came by I would lay the lace down so the tires would roll over it. That would give me a souvenir of this glorious day that the Beatles came to Detroit.

After what seemed like hours (and I think it just may have been because even Nonnie and Orville, my step-grandfather, were about ready to give up and leave) the noise began. Girls screaming, people shouting, everyone was on their feet, and the long-awaited moment had finally come. I was more than ready with my shoelace. I quickly threw it in front of the right front tire as the black limousine passed by. I looked up and all I could see were some vague, shadowy figures behind the dark glass of the limo's windows. I squinted my eyes as hard as I could to try to make out a face, or at least something that I would recognize as Ringo or John. I knew their quirky profiles by heart from the piles of Beatle magazines in my bedroom. In just a few seconds the limo passed by and they were gone. Okay, so, I didn't get even one autograph and Paul McCartney did not smile up at me with sweet, loving eyes letting me know that I was his favorite Beatle fan. Ah ha! I quickly ran over to my dirty shoelace. I now had a one up on all my girlfriends! I could say that I saw John, Paul, George, and Ringo in person and only six feet away! They would never know that the faces had been unrecognizable silhouettes behind the glass. These were bragging rights of immense proportion!

At school on Monday, I told my girlfriends the exciting story and showed them my sacred souvenir shoelace. It turned out that my friends were *somewhat* impressed, but mostly, I think, they were sort of jealous or possibly unbelieving. They didn't want to talk about it much and my story faded away into oblivion. That was just fine. I still had my shoelace.

Chapter 3
Sunshine Came Softly

"When I think of all the worries that people seem to find
And how they're in a hurry to complicate their minds
By chasing after money and dreams that can't come true
I'm glad that we are different, we've better things to do."
—Sung by *The Grass Roots*, 1967

WHEN YOU TAKE A DEEP breath of air and then breathe out, it has a calming and releasing effect on your body. These were the 1950s and '60s. The big war was won, the United States was large and "in charge," and we could just exhale.

Children of the '60s felt this exhalation and sensed that all was well. We began to expand our knowledge, our life without borders, and accept exploration as part of making the world a better place. Either the limits were not there, or we just didn't accept them.

Adults in Kensington Farms worked hard. Mothers were always at home, and cooked and cleaned and worried a lot. Dads were gone all day long. Moms made sure their children were fed, took baths, and had Band-Aids on their knees. Beyond that, they just worried. Was the pork cooked long enough so we didn't get worms? Did you have a poop this morning? Was your bed made and your teethed brushed? Did you wait a half hour after eating before you went swimming? You could drown you know!

Moms also cared a lot about us not bothering them. They must have had important things to do because they always yelled, "Go out and play!" It was their mantra. It was our escape.

In those times, there was a phenomenal calendar. The summers seemed to go on forever. How the calendar has changed over the years I don't understand, but, then, the summers were long and the school years flew by. Summer was the time of full-fledged freedom and Popsicles. The Fourth of July, the ice-cream man, parks, exploring, neighborhood block parties, maybe even a summer vacation—and did I say FREEDOM?

Later in life, when society started talking about not having a summer break from school, I thought, *NO!* How do you ever figure out who you are if you don't have the freedom of summer? How do you know how to get a leech off your leg if you don't have summer? When would you learn to walk the top of the log fence surrounding the Bell's front yard without falling? How do you learn to skateboard, drive a go-cart, or rescue a baby bird if you don't have summer? How do you figure out how to form a "Girls' Union" if you don't have summertime?

The boys in our neighborhood had the thought that they were in charge of everything. Imagine that! Now that I am older and understand that there are elemental differences between the sexes, I suppose the boys were just being who they were. But, at that point in my life, I tried to be the "equalizer." I would watch what was happening between the boys and girls and wonder why in the world the girls would, or could, just accept their fate. "Their fate," as in being the outfield on the baseball team or being the frontline blockers on the football team. Why weren't we allowed in their forts? Why were they so special? My mind could not fathom their arrogance, as I thought it was. My mission, as I understood it, was to bring fairness and understanding between the sexes. Or at least be able to be a "halfback" once in a while.

At a backyard football game, I introduced this concept. The idea did not go over exceptionally well when I explained it to the boys. "Okay, look," I explained, "girls don't always make the best blockers. Actually, you boys would be much better frontline players. You can block really well for us and the girls should be able to run circles around the defense if we had you as protection."

They bought it! There was only one small problem. The girls did not know what the heck they were doing. We fumbled the ball around like Larry, Moe, and Curly would have. Darn, I guess we should have worked that part out first—like formulating plays. The guys, of course, had run offense many times before and sort of knew what they were doing. Well, next time! We will work on it.

At the neighborhood baseball games, the girls started asking to play the infield with some success. The boys were beginning to accept the concept that if they wanted us to play the game, they should allow us to learn the positions.

I called this my "Girls' Union." And, in some way, I think the guys came to appreciate the fact that we were trying to expand ourselves and learn the things that guys were doing. Maybe that was part of their integration into a feminist movement that would have an effect on their lives down the line. They needed to expand and learn also.

I did tend to push my feminist side to the edge, though. In fact, in my mind, I was equal to males—both physically and mentally. Whatever they were doing, I could do it. Why not? I even thought I needed to prove it. A certain reputation developed after I had wrestled most of the boys in the neighborhood.

One day, the boys were sparring with boxing gloves in the Knight's front yard. *Now,* I thought, *that looks like fun!* They paired me up against David Bell. On went the gloves. With some punching at the air and some fancy footwork, I felt like Cassius Clay. After I danced around for a while, looking somewhat like a crazed cockroach, I went in for a contact jab. Punch, jab, then, there was David Bell on the ground! I heard someone say, "Go get his mom!" I don't know if he was fully knocked out, but he sure was dazed. I felt horrible. Not only did I really NOT want to hurt him, I also knew this was the ultimate blow to a guy's ego. A girl punched you out? How does a guy live that one down? David, very successfully, went on to more scholarly pursuits and became the smartest boy in the neighborhood.

I began to rethink my reputation. *Maybe this is not what a twelve-year-old girl needs to be known for.* I liked boys, and they were looking better to me every day. So, it might be possible that hitting them would not be the best way to keep them as friends, especially when you're a girl turning thirteen-years-old and starting to like them in a different sort of way. The Girls' Union was officially dissolved.

Have Bike, Will Travel

From the time you notice the big kids riding their two-wheeler bicycles and you are still tooling around on a baby's trike, the aspiration begins. You realize that you cannot keep riding this safe, familiar, and maneuverable form of transportation. No, you recognize that you must someday graduate to the risky, perilous, fall-at-any-moment means of transport. It is a rite of passage that is contemplated with true desire and with mortal fear.

I was determined that I was not going to step into this unknown venture until I felt secure enough with my capabilities. I took the "wait and see" approach. Not my brother Mark. When he saw Johnny Mikkelsen riding his Schwinn bike with the noisy baseball cards clothespinned onto the spokes, he knew the tricycle had to go. Mark was two years and about ten months old when he started practicing with a girl's bike, and before he was three, he had mastered it.

For his third birthday, mom and dad bought him his first two-wheeler and off he went. He rode with the big kids in the street as I watched from the sidewalk until I mustered the courage to give it a try. I remember dad hanging onto the back of the bike and giving it forward momentum as I struggled to keep my balance. The first few times he let go of the bike I fell, but after a few wobbly attempts, I got the hang of pedaling and keeping the bicycle upright simultaneously. Once you get it, you got it, and your world expands.

In the midst of summer, after all of us had explored the territory within the boundaries we were allowed, one of us would say, "Let's take a bike trip tomorrow." We would coerce our moms into giving in to the idea. Yes, we will stop at all the stop signs. Yes, we will stay on the sidewalks. Yes, we will not go too far.

We ran to our bedrooms to scrounge up some pocket change so we could make the stop at the Dairy Queen on the way home...then we were FREE! We escaped our neighborhood!

We never really knew where we were going, so it truly was an adventure. Sometimes we would go through Tuomy Hills where all the doctors and lawyers lived. It was a very rich, upscale area to us, and we fantasized about what it would be like to live in mansions like these—Tudor-style and European-looking houses with stone or masonry accents, circle driveways, and perfect landscaping. The terrain was rolling hills and curves in the road, unlike our little cracker boxes all in a row.

We'd make our way through the high-class hills and end up on Hill Street, weaving through the University of Michigan buildings and ultimately to State and Liberty Streets. Stopping to explore Middle Earth, the campus "head shop," could be quite eye opening. It was in a big, old house on Liberty Street. They had some fairly strange paraphernalia for purchase, and the long-haired beatnik people in the shops were nicely mellow.

Drifts of incense hung in the air, and words like *mind expanding*, *revolution*, and *peace* were on black light posters. It was the place to be seen, with some cool art thrown in.

The corner record shop had music blasting out of the open doors. They introduced us to The Mamas and The Papas, Bob Dylan, and Joan Baez. The Virginian Restaurant had plates of shoestring french fries that we smothered with ketchup while we played Tommy James & the Shondells on the juke box. As the afternoon rolled on, we strolled past "flower people" in white robes—they were Hare Krishna folks selling flowers. The White Panther movement passed out their buttons and flyers, and sometimes sit-ins were happening at the "Diag," an open grassy area on the University of Michigan campus.

There it was—the beginning of an underground movement. Later it would be known as the "Hippie Generation," a phrase that meant different things to different people. To some, it only meant drugs, communes, and barefoot folks with no jobs or responsibilities. But the movement had much more behind it. It had the word "antidisestablishmentarianism" behind it. At the core, it was what our generation did best. Raise questions. We questioned our society, we questioned our religion, and, especially, we questioned our government. To us, exploring life and what it had to offer was everything. We believed we could improve on anything our parents and the generations before us had formulated. Peace, love, understanding, and making the world a better place—how could you not climb on the train?

Along with that train, we also climbed back on our bikes and meandered our way back to Kensington Farms. Each one of the bike trips we took helped us see the world a little differently and gave us the independence we were seeking. But, for now, it was good to be home again, run in the back door, and say, "Hey, Mom, what's for dinner?"

Chapter 4
Ozzie, Lucy, and The Beaver

"We represent The Lollipop Guild
The Lollipop Guild, The Lollipop Guild
And in the name of The Lollipop Guild
We wish to welcome you to Munchkin Land!"
—Sung by the **Munchkins** in the movie *The Wizard*
of Oz, 1939

THE TELEVISION SET STARTED TO become popular around
1948, but most American families did not have one in their
home until the early 1950s. The picture tubes were massive
compared to what would be the high-digital version fifty years
later. Because she had to be the first with anything new on the
market, my grandma Nonnie's TV set was probably the second

one off the assembly line. When you turned it on, it took time to warm up, and when you turned it off, it had a small bright light in the center of the screen that stayed on for a minute or so. When my brother, Mark, and I spent the night at Nonnie and Orville's house we would pretend that there was a ghost in the TV watching us. Pretty scary stuff when you are about five years old. The TV sat in a wooden cabinet with doors on the front that closed when you weren't watching it. It was definitely part of the living room decor.

Television crept into the lives and families of America. The predictable happy endings on *Ozzie and Harriet, Bachelor Father*, and *The Donna Reed Show* made us think and believe that there should always be peace and goodness abounding. Happy endings made us, well, happy! Ricky Nelson might do something selfish or greedy, but five minutes before the show was to end, he would regret it, confess his sins, and all would be well with the world. Television wanted us to believe that life and happiness was a dad, a mom, at least two kids, and a dog, living happily ever after in a beautiful three-bedroom ranch house.

This newly found invention had a way of bringing families together in the evening after a long day of work and play. So, the traditions began. Sunday night popcorn and Coca Cola and all eyes were on *The Ed Sullivan Show*. The acts that Ed had on his show were so varied you never knew what would be next. Comedians, dancing dogs, ventriloquists, trapeze artists, and rock stars all came to be somebody on *The Ed Sullivan Show*. The biggest night in the history of the show was when Ed hosted the Fab Four. The Sunday night that the Beatles were to be on

The Ed Sullivan Show was a moment in time for most young and crazy fans. It was so exciting to actually see the Fabulous Foursome perform on stage that we sat in front of the TV not mumbling a word. Just staring with perfectly focused eyes in awe of the iconic, young, English rock-and-roll band that we listened to on the radio and 45-rpm records every day.

There were no worries that any television show would be unsuitable for the entire family to view. The only thing my mom worried about was when *Lassie* came on. *Lassie* was a show about a boy, Timmy, and his beautiful collie dog. Lassie was the smartest dog ever! My mom did not worry about the show; she worried about my sister, Carla. Carla was young, about four years old, and took the drama the show created very seriously. She could not bear to see Timmy in distress. We all knew that Lassie would rescue Timmy from being drowned in the well or whatever trouble he was getting into that week. Except for Carla. She took it to heart and would cry until Lassie saved Timmy. By the time the show was over, Carla was a mess. Mom would have to console her and assure her that Timmy was okay now. Bedtime was right after the Lassie show was over, which made it difficult for Mom to put Carla to bed. Other than *Lassie*, television was rated G for all audiences.

The most fun of all was to wake up knowing it was Saturday morning and cartoons would be on TV until noon! The anticipation of four hours of total bliss, a sugar buzz from the Sugar Pops, and just lying around in our pajamas without getting yelled at was pure magic. Wile E. Coyote never caught the Roadrunner, and Sylvester Cat never caught Tweety Bird, but we didn't care. Even to this day, we will sometimes talk like Foghorn Leghorn or Elmer Fudd and reference lines from Popeye, Bugs Bunny, or Yogi Bear. "I ams what I ams and that's all what I ams," "Boy, I say, boy, cut that out, boy," and we are all "smarter than the average bear!"

The clock would strike noon and Mom would announce that we needed to get our stinky bodies up and out of the house. We knew she was just tired of us under her feet, and we had eaten enough Sugar Smacks and Honeycombs to run a marathon, so the fun was over until next Saturday.

After only seeing television in black and white for many years, Grandma Nonnie bought a Motorola color TV in 1964. It was such a new phenomenon that we would go over to Nonnie's house every Sunday to watch Walt Disney's *Wonderful World of Color*. The intro to the show was a moving kaleidoscope of colors that dazzled the eyes. And all eyes were on whatever Walt decided America was going to watch that week.

Every spring the annual *Wizard of Oz* movie was an anticipated event. The showing of the movie just before tornado season every year was planned by the TV industry. It would scare the kids and prompt mothers to give their lecture on what to do in case of a tornado warning. It basically went like this: "Go to the southwest corner of the basement, huddle together, and wait for the house to blow away."

The "boob tube," as we called it, became part of the formation of society and its norms. We saw the world through television. The British invasion, new dances, popular hair styles, and what the new generation was wearing all showed up on *Where the*

Action Is and *American Bandstand. Hey,* we thought, *maybe our parents' generation is **not** where it's at.* TV helped us solidify the thought that WE, the new, the strong, the carriers of the torch, WE now owned the world. TV was an influence that catapulted the kids of the '50s from living in a social bubble to living in a world they wanted to explore. And explore we did.

The proof manifested itself in our positive ideas and forward momentum we thought were better—better than ever! We truly believed in ourselves, sometimes to a fault, but our idealism, individualism, youth, and invincibility were shining through.

Chapter 5
All You Need Is Love

"'Kids are different today,' I hear every mother say
Mother needs something today to calm her down
And though she's not really ill, there's a little yellow pill
She goes running for the shelter of a mother's little helper
And it helps her on her way, gets her through her busy day"
—Sung by The Rolling Stones, 1966

Motherly colloquialisms of the day...

"If you do that one more time..."

We never knew what would happen if we did *it* one more time, but it probably wasn't something we would look forward to.

"Just wait until your father gets home."

This was the absolute final straw. Mothers pulled this threat out as a last resort and we knew it. If we did one more thing that got on her nerves, there could be a very high price to pay.

"You kids are driving me to a nervous breakdown."

This statement was actually comical to us. We snickered, got out of Mom's hair, and figured this was just a sympathy play.

"Go outside and play."

When mothers were tired of their children being in the house, every mother I knew would say this. What it really meant was, "I am tired of your noise and the fact that you are under my feet making messes all over the house. I need a break from you." Sometimes we really wanted to watch TV or just relax around the house. Sometimes we wanted to have friends in our bedroom or in the basement to play. But if Mom said, "Go outside and play," there were no negotiations. You had to meander your way to the door and find something to do outdoors.

With at least thirty kids in close proximity at any given time it usually wasn't difficult to find someone to help you occupy your time when your feet stepped off the porch. I looked across the street to see if Diane was outside, I looked to the right to see if David or Sandy Bell were doing anything, or maybe Betsy or Susie were playing with their Hula-Hoops. If nothing seemed to be happening, we made it happen. "Mother may I?" was a game we played. Four square, dodgeball, hopscotch, red rover, or king of the hill were in the library of activities that we could choose from at any given time. We challenged each other to see who could get the furthest on the log fence that went all the way around the Bell's front yard. You had to do it barefoot to be able to make it the entire distance. Many a sliver was pulled from the bottom of our feet afterward, but, no one cared.

If we were really lucky, Mom would let us walk up Packard Road to Kelsey's Market or Buster's IGA. She would give us a short grocery list of bread, milk, and cigarettes and just enough money to pay for it. Of course she wrote a note to let the cashier know that we were buying them for her, but it still felt pretty grown-up to be buying cigarettes! The two grocery stores were across the street from each other, and maybe a half a mile away on the corner of Packard and Platt roads.

Before it got popular not to be a "litterbug," people threw a lot of things out of their car windows, so the side of the road was kind of like having your own personal garbage dump. If you wanted to get rid of something out of your car, you just tossed it out. No problem, because the bonus in that was finding empty pop bottles in the ditches. The bottle return was two cents and if we could find five bottles, then we had enough money to buy either a Coca Cola, a frozen malted, or a Hershey's chocolate bar. Sometimes it was so difficult to choose which one to buy that it took at least a half an hour to decide.

There were two parks we could walk to. To the east we had Community Park. To the west we had Buhr Park. Community Park was usually the happening place with a full array of playground equipment and a skating rink and shed in the wintertime. Ice skating arm and arm with a boy to the music of the Dave Clark Five blaring from the speaker on top of the warming hut, and playing a game of whiplash where you hold hands with as many people as you can get in a row, skate fast, and try to fling the last person in line off into oblivion, kept us warm in the snowy months. During the summer months, the city arranged to have arts and crafts on special days of the week. Learning to braid colorful flat nylon strings to make a key chain or a necklace that you could put a whistle on was the ultimate coolness. There were contests and games organized by the counselors, and after putting ribbons and bows on my terrier dog Friskie, she won the best in the dog show one year! Buhr Park was mostly a large, open, grassy area where an old, abandoned house and torn-down barn was close to the road. Behind the old buildings were acres of land we could explore. This was a mostly open area and the Fourth of July fireworks were held there. There was a great sledding hill we utilized in the winter because it had a lot of bumps that made it fun to go down on a saucer. Going down the hill on a toboggan was a different situation. This didn't stop us, but it probably looked like we were kernels of popcorn flying everywhere as we struggled to stay on the sled, usually bouncing off along the way.

On a hot summer's day, the coolness of the nearby creek was so inviting but very daring. It was daring because "Don't go down to the creek" was the rule of all the neighborhood mothers. There were *some* obedient children who complied, but for most of us, what mothers did not see, mothers did not know. We were carefree and felt the wind at our backs as we ran along the steep banks of the flowing water and crossed the fallen logs that created small rapids in the current. Pretending to be pirates and swashbuckling our way across the wooden gangplanks placed haphazardly by nature, we dared each other to see who could get across without falling in, and then getting wet on purpose because it felt so good on a hot summer day. It was all the more fun because we weren't even supposed to be there. One day at the creek we found a robin that had a broken wing and brought it home to nurse it back to health. We tried to feed it earthworms but the poor thing didn't want anything to do with us. Instead of helping him, I am sure that we sped up the bird's demise, and we gave Mr. Robin a proper shoebox burial in the backyard feeling like we had done everything we could to help him survive. All that Mom could say was, "You are not supposed to touch birds! You will get lice!" We never got lice, but we did get leeches from the creek a few times. We would pour salt on them and they would fall right off. I remember the daring boys who used matches to burn the leeches to get them off. Salt worked just fine for me.

Most mothers of the day did not care what you were doing as long as you came home in one piece, and on time, for dinner. If one of your siblings was close, or around the house, when dinner was almost ready, Mom would tell them to go outside and get their brothers and sisters. If none of the kids were in sight, then mothers would just yell. They would open the front door and scream our names. We all knew our own mom's voices and high-tailed it home to eat. If we were late for dinner, then Dad would not be happy. We all wanted happy dads because we all knew that a happy dad was, well, a happy life.

Dinnertime had a life of its own. It was a time when the entire family got together and interacted with each other over the supper table. The nightly meal was clearly like our own family board meeting. Dad, being the chairman of the board, would usually lead the topics of our conversations. Sometimes Dad would discuss with Mom things about the house or projects they were planning. Sometimes Dad would ask what we were learning in school or bring up events that we needed to talk about. Sometimes we may have been in trouble that day and we got a talking to. We all had chances to speak up about something if we wanted to, and Dad would listen and give his opinion.

It was a board meeting that served food. Not only were "times a changing" but food was changing too. Like SPAM. A can of SPAM was a staple in the 1950's cupboard. What is SPAM, you ask? I don't really know. But it was a salty, grayish pink, faux meat that was most likely a relic left over from World War II. You either loved it or hated it. The other healthy choice was the famous liver-and-onions-cooked-in-bacon-grease meal. There must have been some well-respected doctor who had proclaimed the nutritional benefits of liver. I can hear him say, "All of the vitamins, minerals, and recommended dose of iron that all growing children need in today's modern world." Not to mention all of the cholesterol and toxins that an animal's filter can provide! Knowing you were going to have to eat liver would lead you to ask your best friend if they could invite you over for dinner. If that didn't work, then dinnertime went something like this:

1. We attempted to chew the pungent, chalky, leather-like pieces of well-done liver.

2. After every bite, we would drink about half of the milk in our glass and then ask for more milk. Thinking we had made a good attempt at eating this health food, we would ask to be excused from the table.

3. Mom would pull out her ultimate tactic to get us to eat all of the food on our plate—GUILT. "There are starving children in China who would love to have the food you are eating," she would say. Our best comeback ever was, "Then go ahead and send it to them," we would reply back in a nice, polite voice.

4. That's when Dad would step in. His tactic was not GUILT. His tactic was an ULTIMATUM. "You either eat the food on your plate or go to your room for the rest of the night."

5. There was daylight left to burn, and none of us wanted to sit in our rooms all night. So, chewing we did, minding our manners, excusing ourselves from the table after finishing everything on our plates, even the canned peas that helped to cover up the residual liver taste.

6. Then we went flying out of the door to erase the memory of the dinner and focus on more important things like skateboarding until the streetlights came on and we had to come in for the night.

Even then I wondered if women raising children and keeping house in that time period were happy. It seemed to me, a life of spotless cleaning, taking care of children, doing laundry, ironing, and fixing meal after meal would leave a longing for more in their souls. As a means to the end, being a housewife, as they were called, seemed to be lacking in the "purpose in life" category. Women gave everything they had to the household and not much appreciation came back their way. It seemed as though women were losing the status they had once had in the family unit, and in effect, some of their self-esteem. This may sound a bit far-fetched, but nonetheless the woman's societal role was in a bit of an adjustment period.

Most women before the '50s had lived a more survival lifestyle. Our moms had grown up in the Depression era and remembered the tough times that most of their families went through. The time it took for everyday chores, such as eating, cleaning, gathering food and water, and taking care of the children took up the greater part of the day. But the modern advances after World War II gave women electric washers and dryers, vacuum cleaners, and canned and frozen food bought at the grocery store instead of preparing the food at harvest time. The purpose of a woman's existence was changing fast, and our moms had to figure out how to "fill in the blanks" of daily living. Many families were moving from farms into towns and suburbs to live in modern houses that were in close proximity to each other. As the television invaded households, networks catered to women with daily soap operas and game shows. I remember watching a TV show called *Queen for a Day*. The ladies chosen to be on the show always had some major catastrophe that had happened to them. As the few women told their own heartbreaking story, with tears streaming down the cheeks, the host of the show would listen, give her a white handkerchief, and then let the audience decide who the winner should be. The winner was decided by the "Applause-O-Meter." The woman with the loudest applause was ushered to the throne and pronounced "Queen for a Day." She was wrapped in a royal velvet robe, crowned with a shimmering tiara, and given a dozen red roses. The grand prize was something that would help to make her life better, such as a wheelchair for her son, or a hearing aid for her mother, or perhaps a washing machine. Pretty dramatic stuff!

Other than watching daytime TV, moms would get together for coffee and gossip, play bridge, have Tupperware parties, and read *Life* magazine. Our moms searched for their purpose in different ways. Some mothers found joy in being an excellent cook, some in trying to be the most beautiful of all ladies on the block, and some in being an intellectual. My mother's accepted mission was to have the cleanest house on the block. I have memories of Mom vacuuming at midnight and then complaining the next day about how hard she worked to keep our house looking its best. She certainly attained her goal, and I was proud to have the most meticulously kept house in the neighborhood, or even within the city of Ann Arbor.

The other thing my mom was really great at was worrying about us. If we complained, or if she thought that we were sick, it was off to the doctor we went. We would come home with a prescribed remedy and Mom would proclaim our ailment as the worst diagnosis that it could be. When Mark and I were about eight and nine years old, we acquired a plethora of planter warts on our feet. Both of us at the very same time! We had at least ten warts on the bottom of each foot. Mom to the rescue! She called the doctor and came back with a bottle of something that looked like iodine and smelled worse. The directions, Mom declared, was to pour this orange substance onto our warts, and at the same time poke them with a toothpick. It was, as we experienced, an extreme form of torture. We screamed and cried and tried to run away from her, but to no avail. The doctor's directions had to be followed, and her goal was to make us wart-less. Our goal was to escape these nightly torture sessions. One night, Mark and I decided to scream so much that Mom could not possibly handle performing this medical nightmare any longer. We succeeded by throwing the biggest conniption fit imaginable. When the toothpick came close to our feet, we would let out big moans. We screamed loudly as the pick hit the wart, and we did not let up as she applied the medicine. We whimpered pathetically afterward. The next night we waited. No signs of toothpicks or the medicine bottle. Mom never mentioned having us go through the ordeal again, except I heard her mumbling something about her not knowing how our warts would ever go away. Whether it was the medicine or just time, the warts miraculously went away.

Brother Doug was the youngest of us all and the baby of the family in all ways. Of course he had a given name, Douglas Carl, but we just called him Dougie Boo Boo. Mom and Dad brought him home from the hospital when I was in the second grade, and for me it was love at first sight. We played peek-a-boo and I would blow air into his belly to make noises and he would laugh. I would lie on my back on the floor, put him on my feet, and tell him he was an airplane. Doug loved the attention he received as the baby and was happy and ready to do anything and everything we threw at him. He was cute, charismatic, and a bundle of energy! But Doug's first few years of life were consumed with being sick. Mom worried. She took him to the doctor with ear infections, stomach problems, and allergies. I think she worried so much that she worried him well. Doug grew into a handsome, strong man.

My dad always said, "You know, your mom would give her life for any of you kids." As a child it made me feel good to know that Mom would go to the ends of the earth to make sure we were safe and healthy. Her worry was her form of love, and it was comforting to know that Mom had my back.

During the 1950s and '60s, my thoughts on how society viewed and portrayed women seemed that it was evolving into the *invisibility* of the female's worth. The role of the woman in America was changing. No longer did she need to tend the garden and milk the cow in order to survive. Because the world was changing with every new invention, their roles were evolving, and the identity of the gender had to again prove its relevance to the societal whole. The only educated opportunity for women in the work place, as I saw it back in that era, was to be a teacher, a secretary, a librarian, or a nurse. These seemed to be the only choices at the time. Many of the young baby boomer women growing up and looking at their future knew that there needed to be more to life than just the daily chores. It spawned a rationale in thinking that there should be more equality, which really meant respect, between men and women.

Chapter 6
Draggin' the Line

*"Please don't mistake me or try to make me the
shadow of anybody else
I ain't the him or her you think I am, I'm just trying
hard to be myself
Oh, society's goal is to be part of the whole. That may
sound good to you, not to me. Let me be, let me be…"*
—Sung by *The Turtles*, 1966

THE YEAR WE MOVED TO the neighborhood, my brother Mark
was a little over two years old, and I was three and a half. Being
fairly normal youngsters, we needed to explore our new territory.
Our boundaries were yet obscure to us, and I don't think we even
knew what parameters we were supposed to stick to, so Mark and

I struck out on an adventure traveling down Cranbrook Road to check out the lay of the land. Many of the neighbors were also just moving in, and I recall that there were a lot of trash items set out at the curb for pickup that day. I don't know which one of us spotted the can of beautiful robin-egg-blue paint, but it was surely something to investigate. One thing led to another, and we ended up painting each other with the oil-based blue paint. I think we were the original Smurfs! Finally, making our way back home, we saw Mom waiting in the driveway for us. The look on her face and the words coming out of her mouth soon made us understand the word *fear*.

At three years old, I am sure that I had already heard my share of words that parents can say but words we knew we were not allowed to say, but I don't think I was prepared for this. This time, the words came flying at me as they came spewing out from my temporarily possessed mother. She was overcome with anger, frustration, and basically not knowing what to do. What DO you do with painted children? This possibility had not been covered in the Dr. Spock child-rearing books.

We were tossed into steel laundry tubs in the basement and doused repeatedly with turpentine. Some remnants of the dirty words were still drifting in the air, but eventually Mom cooled down and said, "You just wait until your father gets home." From that time on, I knew that Mom could always trump me. I knew that as soon as my father got home I would be on the witness stand with two prosecutors and no defense attorney. The lesson learned was that having fun could sometimes have consequences.

No one told us how to have fun; we could figure it out on our own. Four children on car trips could be very challenging. Kids can be very annoying if you make them sit still for very long. They usually like to kick the backs of the front car seats or cry for no reason, but without any seat belts to strap us in, at least it wasn't too difficult to move around the car. Dad bought an old, black, DeSoto automobile. Three-speed on the column and rusted holes in the back seat floorboard, entertainment abounded. Mark and I would get on the floor, peer through the holes, and watch the pavement go by. "I saw a stone!" "I saw some gum!" we would announce as Mom drove down the road. On nightly trips, when we were a little more tired from the day, we had a bevy of songs to sing. "The Farmer in the Dell," "Three Blind Mice," "Sing a Song of Sixpence," and "Mary Had a Little Lamb" were tunes we could belt out.

In those days, if you left your kids in the car on a hot summer's day, no one got arrested. Honestly. Well, at least if the windows were down. We only had one family car, which was nothing unusual, and Mom would take Dad to work in order to have the car to run errands. Mom did not need us in the store, so we usually were told to behave until she returned. The thrill of being naughty and not getting caught was exhilarating. We made up games of yelling at people walking by and then diving to the floorboard so they couldn't see us. We thought that was pretty funny. Or Mark would pretend he was driving the car and turn the steering wheel as far as he could both ways. On one such occasion, he stretched his little legs to use the accelerator as well as the brake and the clutch. Even though he couldn't even see over the dashboard, it didn't matter; we were having fun pretending. When we saw Mom coming out of the store, we sat like perfect children. Mom would ask, "What are you two doing?"

The answer was always, "Nothing."

The ignition would turn *Ruuh-ruh-ruh.* "Why won't this car start?" she'd say. Mom was getting mad now. Mom found a man to help her get the car started, and we heard a lot of, "If you kids ever do this again…" We knew we would basically be dead.

Because there was only sixteen months between our ages, Mark and I were cohorts in mayhem. Getting in trouble wasn't too much of a big deal to us though. That is, unless Dad was home.

When we weren't fighting each other, we joined forces and made havoc for Mom. We'd chase each other, screaming as we played cowboys and Indians, cops and robbers, running throughout the house, and crashing into walls. It would end up with Mom yelling, "Do you want a spanking? If you don't quit it I'm getting the belt out!" We had a broom closet no more than about ten inches wide, just enough room for a broom, dustpan, and a place to hang up a nice leather belt. Mom never used it and we knew this. So we just kept doing whatever we were doing until she had reached the end of her rope and she'd scream, "Go into your rooms right now and just wait until your father gets home!"

Oh, boy. Now we knew we had crossed over the line. Mom was officially mad and there was no recourse to be had. Off to our rooms we went. In our rooms, we had formed a communication system somewhat like Morse code. It was a bit comforting to know that we were both in trouble together. Although there was no safety in numbers, it did make it better to share in our punishment. Mark would knock two times on the wall between our rooms, and I would knock back four times, meaning, "We are in trouble." He would knock back two more times, saying, "So what?" or "Oh well." I think that's what it meant, because that is exactly what he would have said.

Then, the back door opened and we knew the GIANT was home. We usually had about a 50-50 chance of not really getting too much reprimand from Dad. Dad worked very physical jobs and when he got home, he was ready to take a shower, relax, and have supper. The last thing he wanted to do was to deal with yelling at, spanking, or otherwise punishing kids. After Mom would fill him in on our shenanigans of the day, he would finally come into our rooms and ask us why we were not minding our mother. We would always say, "I don't know." Then he would either say, "Well, then, don't ever do it again" or "Well, maybe after supper you better just go back to your rooms" or the dreaded "Well, I think I better get the belt."

I only remember getting spanked three or four times in my life. The belt from the broom closet would come out, and I felt like the end of my life was now approaching. Two swats on the buttocks—*whack, whack*—and then it was over. But those were the longest five seconds of my life. One time I put a book in my pants to cover my butt. I actually thought he might not notice or have sympathy for me because I was so afraid. Of course it was to no avail. I didn't fool him at all and it only made him a bit madder. Foiled again! I think I got three swats that time instead of two.

Both my brother and I would cry our eyes out, and I would think thoughts of running away or how sorry my grandparents would feel for me if they knew I had just been spanked. Nonnie would always take our sides when we were in trouble. She'd feel sorry for me! But by the next day all was forgotten and we were back to our rambunctious selves again. We didn't question whether or not our parents loved us; we knew they did. We didn't think it was child brutality. The fact was, every kid in the neighborhood was spanked or disciplined by their parents. We accepted it and knew deep down that it was for our own good.

Our parents were always parents. They didn't even pretend to be our friends. Compliments and encouragement came in very small doses. Parents didn't go around telling their kids how wonderful they thought they were. If you were being a slacker, they were not afraid to tell you. If you were not doing well at school, they made you do better or you were sent to summer school.

To us, our parents were symbols of authority and the enforcers of the law. We feared them, but we were not afraid of them, at least not if we were staying within the boundaries they created for us. It was a matter of respect that we knew we should have for them. The fear came from knowing what could happen if we stepped too far out of line. Sure, all of the kids in the neighborhood complained about it to the other kids when they had to stay indoors all day and couldn't go out and play, but we knew that consequences would happen for unacceptable behavior and we had to "suck it up." Back then, if we had gone to school and told the teachers that our parents were mean because they spanked us, the teacher would have said, "So, what did you do?" There really was no way around *not* taking responsibility for our actions. No coddling. No sympathy. We were forced to pull the bootstraps up and grow up.

Chapter 7
Where Were You?

"Didn't you love the things that they stood for?
Didn't they try to find some good for you and me?
And, we'll be free someday soon, it's gonna be one day.
Abraham, Martin, and John."
—**Sung by** *Dion,* **1968**

IT WAS A GREAT DAY at school. The fourth-grade Girl Scouts were getting out of class early to go on a field trip to the Botanical Gardens. The Girl Scout leader, Mrs. Kiddon, and a few other moms, picked us up at school and off we went to see the flora at the newly constructed University of Michigan Botanical Gardens Greenhouse. I remember it being a sunny afternoon, a bit brisk, but a nice day for a November outing in Michigan.

The greenhouse was warm as we strolled through the various types of plants organized by their genera and geographical prominence. There were the South American jungle plants, the desert cacti, the familiar northern climate varieties of plants, tropical palm trees, and the most interesting of all, the Venus Fly Trap. It was the very first time I saw a plant eat a fly! When we walked by a species called a Dieffenbachia, I recognized it immediately. My mom was always trying to keep one alive and growing in our living room.

Even though it was November, we walked outdoors for a while to look at the autumn gardens, but we were happy to scramble back into Mrs. Kiddon's car and get out of the cold. As her sedan pulled out of the driveway of the gardens, a man motioned for us to pull over. Mrs. Kiddon rolled her window down and the man quietly talked to her with a very serious look on his face. In the back seat, the giggling girls began to realize the sudden mood change, and we all perked our ears. As she rolled up the car window, Mrs. Kiddon looked visibly concerned. She turned to girls and said, "President Kennedy has been shot. We do not know if he is still alive or not."

We looked at each other in disbelief and a veil of silence fell over the car. The president of the United States had been shot. What would happen to our country now? Who could ever take John F. Kennedy's place? How could this be? He had been president for less than two years, but in that short span of time he had won over the hearts and souls of Americans. *Who in the world would ever want to kill him?* I thought.

I just wanted to get home. I wanted to run into my house and have Walter Cronkite tell me that everything would be okay, the president was going to recover, and life would go on just as before. But, no, there was my mom, her eyes fixated on the television. I could tell from her expression it wasn't good news. She said, "He's dead. President Kennedy has been shot." I had to ask if she was certain that he really was dead. I did not want to believe it. I joined her in front of the TV and there we sat for days watching everything the news could tell us. The drama escalated when Lee Harvey Oswald, the suspected killer, was shot by a mobster, Jack Ruby. Not only did Kennedy's killer get shot, it happened in front of all of America as the major networks were filming the transfer of Oswald from the Dallas Police Headquarters to the county jail.

Kennedy's assassination happened on a Friday, so we were consumed with the events for the whole weekend. School was cancelled for Monday, and the reality sunk in as we watched the funeral. I remember trying to go outside and play and forget about it for a while, but there was an inescapable sadness in the air. The grieving had to happen.

If you ask anyone who lived in the United States during that time period, "Where were you and what were you doing when you found out that JFK was shot?" they will tell you at length exactly where they were and how they reacted when they heard the news.

The Camelot era of the Kennedys ended with three-year-old little "John-John" saluting his father's casket as the horse-drawn caisson passed by. That gesture showed bravery, respect, and a maturity that for one more time captured the hearts of America.

As Camelot faded into the sunset, the harsher realities in our country stepped up to the forefront—an escalating war, racial tensions, and a generation coming of age that was not afraid to speak their minds. There was no going back.

Chapter 8
On a Summer's Day

*"You don't know how many times I've wished that I
could hold you
You don't know how many times I've wished that I
could mold you into someone
Who could cherish me as much as I cherish you."*
—**Sung by** *The Association, 1966*

KIDS NEED A PLACE THEY can escape to, a place to express themselves, a place of discovery, and a place to let it all hang out. That place was "The Barn." After the farmer and his wife moved out of the farmhouse, the Ward family moved in. They were a young family with kids who were nice enough to allow the entire subdivision clan to play in their barn anytime we wanted to. I never remember an adult being anywhere near the barn, and even though the farmhouse was steps away from the large, rolling barn doors we never worried that Mrs. Ward would walk in on our play.

"The Barn" was really a barn. It had an upper hay loft with a hole in the floor for throwing the hay bales down to the main floor. It had stalls for animals, although the only animals in the barn were the rowdy neighborhood kids. There were a few musty rooms here and there, a large open area in the front part of the barn, doors on the backside, large rolling doors on the front side, and windows all around. It was the perfect hide-and-go-seek spot, and we made excellent use of it.

As we got older, it became a place where boys could get away with kissing girls. It was always the talk of the neighborhood gang if "so and so" went to the barn with "so and so." We knew what they were doing and we usually spied on them.

Things never got too heavy in the barn though. "Apple, peaches, pumpkin pie, who's not ready holler 'I'" was what we'd yell after counting to fifty while everyone hid. I don't remember anyone getting hurt, but I wonder why, as I think about how we always ran from the person trying to find us. We were jumping down the hayloft chute to the first floor, diving behind the old, dirty sofa, and climbing over the animal stall walls to escape the "finder," because if the finder tagged us then we were out of the game.

After a few rounds of hide-and-seek, we would organize a baseball game in the field that was once a cornfield. There were still furrows from the plow that had long-ago turned the earth in the springtime. Since the time the farmer had moved, no plows, or any other landscaping machines had moved the dirt. The infield had been flattened down somewhat throughout the years, but the outfield was downright dangerous ground.

The girls were definitely outfield material, and the guys got all of the action in the infield. When it came time for the girls to get their turn at bat, the boys always looked at us, rolled their eyes, and moved in slowly on the infield to let us know they did not expect much. When one of us girls did hit a fly ball over their heads, the boys would scramble backward looking a little more respectful on the way back in with the ball. Mostly, we were just glad the boys let us play.

Dream Lover

In those days, neighborhoods were fairly secluded from each other, with lines of entry points that we were all aware of. You did not venture into another neighborhood unless you had a friend who got you in. My buddy Claire was my ticket into the man of my dreams' neighborhood. I would ask her for daily updates on what Mike was doing, if he was "going" with any other girls, or anything else she could tell me to fill me in on his life. When I could get over to her house, being that it was a little over a mile away, I would ask her if we could take walks past his house so he would then see us and long to come out and talk to us, or maybe he would be outside and we could strike up a conversation. I just wanted to get a glimpse of him, drool over him, and daydream the summer day away. What would it be like to marry him, to spend eternity gazing into his eyes, to have him hold me in his arms? He was so cool. He was a drummer in what we called a "garage band." *The Take Five* played at school dances and they had a lot of groupies. I was one of them. And, did I mention, Mike was *so* cool?

Finally, after months, possibly years, of occupying my brain with way too many puppy-love thoughts, Mike called me on the telephone. Mike wanted to know if he could come over and we could hang out. My mouth sputtered, "Uh ... sure," and then my heart rose, sank, fluttered, and then stopped. I was excited, nervous, even more nervous, then elated.

I told the entire neighborhood about it and we made the game plan. Mike and I would talk for a while and then someone would suggest that we go to the barn and hang out. I couldn't believe it! Mike was coming over to see me, and all of the kids on the block were helping me plan and strategize. For one spontaneous, fleeting moment, it seemed that all of the neighborhood kids were working with me on this. Could it be real? All of my dreams were coming true in one day!

When Mike rode up on his five-speed Schwinn bike, it played out like clockwork. The boys in the neighborhood played coy as Michael and I sat on the curb and talked. The Rose boys, my brother Mark, and a couple of others rode up on their bikes and suggested we could all go over to the barn. "Sure, that sounds great," said Mike. Now I was really stuck. I *had* to go to the barn with my dream lover. There was no choice, just destiny.

I felt as if I was walking down the wedding aisle as we strolled across the bumpy furrows of the farmer's field. *There is no turning back now,* I thought. Would I let him kiss me? Yes, I decided quickly, but nothing else, only a kiss. Or maybe two.

We migrated to an old sofa on the ground level of the barn. Mike sat down and said, "Come and sit down by me." *Okay,* I thought, *I can do that.* Small talk, then Mike's arm around my shoulder, then, then it came, a couple of nice, sweet, perfectly placed pecks on my lips. *Whew, I can do this,* I thought. As his lips met mine once again, I heard something from the direction of the window across from us. Noise and laughter outside of the barn as the neighborhood boys let it be known that they were spying on us. Those weirdos! I thought they were working with me on this one. But now I could see it was all a plot! They had turned back into the boys I really knew.

Mike and I jumped from the sofa and went outside to the side of the barn where the boys were flying away on their bikes. "I'll see you in a couple weeks when school starts," said Mike. "That sounds great," I said back. It would be our year as ninth graders and our final year at Tappan Junior High School. I was excited that we were the upperclassmen and would be able to rule the school for one year.

September came, Mike played football, played in his band, and had plenty of groupies. He didn't seem to have much time or interest for me. I held a torch for him the entire school year, but the unrequited love slowly faded into reality, and the flame extinguished. For years afterward, when I would drive past his home, I wondered where he was now, what he was doing, and how life may have unfolded for him. Mike was my first puppy love and an awakening that life doesn't always turn out the way you dream it. But, alas, they were wonderful dreams.

Chapter 9
Free, Free, Free

"Half-wracked prejudice leaped forth
'Rip down all hate,' I screamed.
Lies that life is black and white spoke from my skull,
I dreamed
Romantic flanks of musketeers, foundation deep
somehow.
Ah, but I was so much older then, I'm younger than
that now."
—**Sung by** *The Byrds, 1967*

WHEN YOU SENSE THAT YOUR entire life is ahead of you, the choices presented to you seem endless. You have the freedom to choose. You have the freedom to make mistakes and recover from them. As your life progresses, both theoretically and mathematically, your time runs out. Your freedom to make choices seems narrower and riskier. Is that what freedom is? Having time on your side and the luxury to change course and start anew. Is that what it means to be free?

"Freedom" as a topic could lead to endless discussion of experiences, theory, and philosophy, but during the second half of the 1960s, *freedom* became a word that the American youth clung to and embraced with gusto. We were able to feel the freedom to explore because our generation reaped the benefits of many hardworking people who, before us, had scrimped and saved, followed society's rules, and wanted to make the world a better place. We wanted to make the world a better place also, but, just in a different way. We didn't see that following all of the social norms was our way to improve humanity. We thought that thinking outside of the box, showing individuality, and believing in the brightness of the future of the world was our positive force. Because we were young our choices were many. But it also seemed as though we felt an urgency to live life to the fullest, to follow a different path, and to explore the world before us. We thought humans should get along much better than they had been, and we should all give peace a chance. Communes became a popular idea along with food cooperatives and joining the Peace Corps. Parents were shaking their heads. Sons and daughters seemed to be choosing lifestyles that were not congruent with the values their generation had tried to instill in us. How can my daughter be working on an organic farm when she should be going to college? Why did my son go to California to work odd jobs when he could be helping with the family business? Why would my children want to live in a tent in Arizona when they have a perfectly good bed at home? What's the matter with kids today? *Antidisestablishmentarianism* was said to be the longest word in the dictionary in those days. We thought it was a pretty cool word. We spelled it, and said it as fast as we could and thought it meant something like "being against the status quo" (which it didn't!). It felt very rebellious to say it though. The Almighty Creator, or whatever force you may believe in, set up the people in this era to be willing to question, explore, and believe in a forward momentum on a different plane of life. I suppose, part of it was a culmination of prosperity that allowed for the freedom to do it. We looked at that freedom and ran with it. No holding back. We were ready for the mental freedom to put our mark on the earth.

"Freedom's just another word for nothin' left to lose
Nothin', it ain't nothin' honey, if it ain't free."
—Sung by *Janis Joplin, 1970*

Chapter 10
Time Has Come Today

"There's battle lines being drawn
Nobody's right if everybody's wrong
Young people speaking their minds
Getting so much resistance far behind."
—Sung by *Buffalo Springfield, 1967*

THE DECADE AFTER WORLD WAR II set a societal tone of
uniformity, cooperation, achievement, and of *façades*. The façade
was the illusion of a possibility of perfectionism in everyday life.
I am referring to the 1950s. The post-World War II generation
had the immense desire for the perfect house, the perfect
family, and the perfect future. After the Great Depression and
the Great War, society felt the need to strive for goodness and

normalcy in their lives. They needed to get back on track with a forward momentum. I use the term loosely, but I call it the Plastic Decade. Plastic as a material became the resin of choice in the '50s with every gadget being made with the durable, non-decomposing substance. Women threw Tupperware parties and bought MelMac dish sets at the grocery store, whichever plate or cup was the weekly featured item. Plastic wrap and plastic baggies were much more durable than waxed paper. Transistor radios, Frisbees, Hula-Hoops, Barbie dolls ... we loved our plastic. The Plastic Decade seemed to symbolize conformity and non-individualism in society.

Then, it happened. The children of the post-war generation were beginning to come of age. The reality is that because those children did not live through the drastic experiences of their parents, they could not understand the grand façade. While it is true that rarely does any generation willingly conform to the one before it, to say the boomer generation wanted anything remotely resembling their parents' generation would be greatly stretching the truth.

The truth was that we could not understand why our parents followed all the social norms and why they were so afraid of being different. We, the next generation, had decided to take the bull by the horns and change the world. Individuality and freedom was our war cry. The changes that happened amongst the youth were not slow, nor were they subtle. Even then, I felt a bit of remorse for the generation that had raised me. Everything that seemed proper and good to them was being thrown out the window. The youth were growing their hair long, playing rock and roll, wearing crazy bell bottoms, and wanted their bedrooms painted in psychedelic colors. What in the world was happening and where do parents draw the line? They didn't have a clue.

In a last-ditch attempt to get my brother to see how ridiculous his "Beatle" haircut was, one morning my dad came to breakfast with what hair he had left on his head combed down straight forward on his forehead. It was about the most hilarious thing we had ever seen! Not only did it *not* convince my brother to get a Princeton cut, it probably encouraged him to grow his hair even longer.

When I think about a turning point, or a moment in time, when the world seemed to move in a very different direction, it was the summer of '67. Change was in the air. It was a long, hot, summer of racial riots, an escalating war, protests on campuses, questioning of the government, and some really fabulous music on the radio. Change was in the air.

Sitting on the sofa at my best friend's house, Diane and I were reading the latest *Life* magazine with the Israeli War featured on the cover, but it was the article on the Beatles that spiked our interest. John Lennon was dating Yoko Ono, and Paul McCartney was admittedly taking drugs. What in the world was happening out there? Even the Beatles were changing. Their music had become increasingly psychedelic with underlying themes. John and Yoko were vocal about what was wrong with the world, so we listened. Peace and love seemed like the better option than the wars and riots going on around us. Although, to some, the peace and love mantra were becoming synonymous with the drug culture, but the Peace Movement permeated our attitudes and formulated our beliefs with, or without, the drugs. The energy of the Hippie culture, as it began to be called, stemmed from the basis of peace, love, and freedom. It sounds idealistic, and it was, but we didn't care. We believed in the positive forward momentum of it. Social norms were evolving with this next generation and the Age of Innocence made way for the Dawning of Aquarius.

At Tappan Junior High School, the ninth graders were king of the mountain. Next year in high school we would drop directly to the bottom of the heap, but for one glorious year, we were pseudo upperclassmen. What started out in seventh grade with kilt skirts and knee-high socks, ended up in ninth grade with miniskirts and shoes called "flats" of every color. Classic style had turned mod. The summer of '67 was the summer before our final year at Tappan Junior High. The seven-minute version of The Doors' song "Light my Fire," "White Rabbit" by Jefferson Airplane, and "Let's Live for Today" by The Grass Roots were the songs of the summer. The new downtown club for teens, The 5th Dimension, was the perfect place to be seen. The club held "The Battle of the Bands," challenging local bands to come and show their stuff. There would be three or four bands all playing at the same time. Usually the loudest band won, but no one cared, we just liked it all! Jimi Hendrix played The 5th, Bob Seger's bands were one of the regulars, and when Diane and I heard that The MC5 had a gig at the club, we had to be there!

Although Diane and I may have been the upperclassmen at school, walking into The 5th Dimension made us feel, at best, miniscule. I said, "Let's stick together," as we meandered our way through the moving sea of teens. I did not want to get separated and have to be on my own in this place of mayhem.

We saw a few of our friends from school, which gave us some comfort, but most of the crowd was older than us. We mingled through the masses as the excitement built. We were going to see the hippest band ever, The MC5, perform live on stage! As the band set up and finally got on stage, the frenzy built and Diane and I, along with everyone else, tried to get as close to the band as we could. The noise began—loud, raucous, screaming rock. I knew at that moment I was stepping away from any sense of "normal" I had tried to pretend this was.

Music had captured the youth and held them hostage with a power that changed a generation. The music gave us direction; we listened and believed. It told us what was wrong with the world and how we should change it.

The amps pushed out the loud and pounding beats as we tried to look cool and groove with the music. The MC5 aligned its loyalties and convictions with John Sinclair and the White Panther Party. It was a cause that seemed, at that time, to start out with good intentions of supporting the Black Panther cause. The political slant of The MC5 band was definitely part of their aura, and they did not hide the fact they were very much against the Vietnam War and the "Establishment." So, along with enjoying their music we got indoctrinated into the political mind-set that was permeating young minds.

My young brain that had not accepted the order of society yet, and was idealistic, truly wanted to believe that our generation would lead the world into a better era. I wasn't exactly sure how we were going to accomplish this, but I wanted to help in any way I could. I was willing to "Trick or Treat for UNICEF" or read *The Prophet* by Kahlil Gibran or even listen to the *self-proclaimed* prophets preaching from the street corners to try to understand how to figure out a better way forward. In 1967, walking down State Street in Ann Arbor was the best place to find your own personal cause du jour. In fact, walking onto the University of Michigan campus at that time was an entrenchment into the subcultures of the day. You never knew what influence was going to reach out and grab you. Walking through the "Diag," a large, grassy area along State Street where students congregated for a sit-in, or to get high, or both, could be as enlightening as watching the nightly news. Protests against the Vietnam War were common place. The Hare Krishna followers would be on the corner of State and Liberty selling flowers as music floated out of the record store with sounds of Judy Collins, Bob Dylan, and The Young Rascals. So, as I listened to a man on a raised step of a store promoting the ideals of the White Panther Party, I thought, *This is an idea I can accept. What could be wrong with equality for all races and the betterment of society?* I accepted his button and proudly pinned it to my leather purse. As they say, naivety is bliss.

A year or so later, I realized the White Panthers were becoming a less than peaceful party. My friend Sue really wanted my button so I gave it up. It looked much better on her jean jacket anyway.

It was *The Summer of Love*, a time of believing and a definitive time of change for the youth, for America, and especially for the bewildered parents of the day. With my idealism very much intact, I was ready to absorb the world.

Chapter 11
Come to Naught

"He's five feet two and he's six foot four
He fights with missiles and with spears
He's all of thirty-one and he's only seventeen
He's been a soldier for a thousand years."
—Sung by *Buffy Sainte-Marie, 1964*

IN ELEMENTARY SCHOOL, ON EVERY Friday afternoon, teachers would hand out the *Weekly Reader*. The *Weekly Reader* was like a mini newspaper, about four pages, of news and current events written for different grade levels and in a way that children could enjoy reading it. It would have some world news, some national news, a puzzle or two for fun, and trivia and facts that kids could relate to. On a certain Friday afternoon, Mr. Smith, my sixth-grade teacher, plopped the latest edition on my desk. On the front cover, center section, was a small news article that told me that America was sending more soldiers to a place called Vietnam. The article also said that we had been sending soldiers there since 1961. This was now 1964, and I had never heard this news before. I was astonished. At dinner that night I asked my dad, "Dad, did you know that we are fighting a war in a place called Vietnam?"

"Yes, I did know that," he said.

"So, why did no one ever tell me?" I blurted out. I was a little perturbed. How can our country be at war and nobody ever told me? It amazed me that America could send our military to fight a war and it seemed as if it was no big deal to anyone. I thought, *I better start paying attention!*

Of course, the war escalated from there. I believe our parents really tried to support the reasons that we were in Vietnam, and they trusted the government to make the right decisions. For heaven's sake, we had fought World War II for good causes and it put the United States on top of the existing world order. I am sure they could not fathom that our governmental leaders would get us into a war without good reasons. I wanted to believe that too.

As time went on, though, more and more young men and women were being killed and it became very personal. Families were sending their children to a questionable war and many were not returning. When I was fifteen, my friend Chuck Brown went to Vietnam. He didn't make it home alive. I know that his parents, or any of his family, were never the same without Chuck. I could see it in Mr. Brown's eyes as I waitressed at the counter of the local

Dog 'n' Suds Diner. Life had been drawn out of him, and as I took his lunch order I only saw sadness and maybe a bit of anger. This senseless war had taken his son from him.

At an anti-war demonstration on the U of M campus, someone gave me a silver metal MIA (missing in action) bracelet. The bracelets they handed out had the names of soldiers who were either missing in action or were POWs (prisoners of war). These crescent-shaped bands were handed out to help gain focus on the thousands of people missing in battle or were actual known prisoners. We were told to pray for the person on the bracelet we had been given, think of them daily, and not forget the soldiers who were fighting for us. I tried to remember to do that daily. I wondered the whereabouts of this man I was given the responsibility to pray for. Was he alive, or was I praying for naught? Some days it felt good to pray for him, and on other days it seemed useless. But I prayed.

I never found out what happened to him and eventually I forgot his name because I willingly passed the bracelet over to a friend who wanted it. It was her turn to pray. I pray that he made it home safely to his family.

The men I know, or have known, who did return from Vietnam, needless to say, were strongly impacted from their experience. Many, I am sure, felt the uselessness, the waste of human lives, and the horrendous uncertainty of what would happen to them. I really wanted to hear their stories of what they went through, but I have discovered that very few will talk about it. They do not want to relive it. From what smidgen I have ever gathered, it was a time of survival for them, moment to moment, not knowing the situation or command that could come next. Many soldiers saw horrendous actions and situations in 'Nam. Nothing they cared to remember.

The Saturday night in 1973 when the cease fire began in Hanoi, I was in Bimbo's restaurant. When the rock-'n'-roll band announced the cease fire had been signed by President Nixon, the crowd went crazy. Everyone was hugging and yelling and dancing. It felt as though a tremendous burden was lifted from my being. Many pitchers of beer were drawn that night. It had been a long haul, too long, and with too many lives lost. We were tired of our friends dying "over there." Period.

Chapter 12
The Age of Destruction

"It seems to me such an easy, easy, thing this would be, why can't you and me learn to love one another All the world over, so easy to see, people everywhere just wanna be free I can't understand it, so simple to me, people everywhere just got to be free."
—Sung by *The Young Rascals*, 1968

EVEN THOUGH THE PEACE MOVEMENT and the protests against the Vietnam War were getting legs, the racial tensions were escalating. Newark, New Jersey, and other major cities in the United States were having what they were calling race riots. During the summer of 1967, and so close to our little world,

Detroit had their own. When the news announced that a large part of the city of Detroit was burning and people were being killed in the streets, I wondered if the violence of the riots would continue on to Ann Arbor.

That thought was scary. Our safe and quiet neighborhood felt somewhat threatened. I thought it through, and my rationale decided that the riots would have to go through Ypsilanti first, and surely they would stop before it all came this far! And, if they somehow did get this far, my dad would find a safe haven for us somewhere. It sure was nice to have adults who would take care of me. My sheltered life was manifesting itself.

In about a week, the riot scene in Detroit had been quieted by the soldiers who were sent in along with the police and fire departments of the city. Forty-three people died and 1,189 were injured in the riots. The nightly news covered it in depth and sometimes it felt as though Armageddon was upon us. On a Sunday afternoon, a couple of weeks later, my dad announced we were going to drive into Detroit to see the damaged remains of the aftermath. I was a bit astonished that he could even suggest this! Wouldn't he be putting his beloved family in harm's way? My imagination saw smoldering buildings and soldiers with guns waiting to shoot at any moving target.

Into the car we went, driving away from our dear, safe, Cranbrook neighborhood. I sat in the back seat of the car with curiosity and anxiety playing against each other. It was a hot August day, but as we neared the riot area, I rolled up my rear car window and pushed down the lock on the door. For quite a few blocks the burned-out buildings and glassless windows of shops depicted the remnants of a war zone. I could only imagine what it might feel like to be on these streets when the National Guard tanks were rolling down them. My hope and my prayer that day was that this was not a sign of more unrest to come. But the tensions and chaos continued all that summer. Within the next year, we tragically lost our great leaders Bobby Kennedy and Martin Luther King Jr., with the angst continuing on over the next few years to the Kent State University shootings in 1970.

Can't there be some compromise? I thought. *Why can't we all get along and be happy? Why do people **want** strife in their lives?* My very naïve thoughts seemed reasonable to me at the time, although, I learned later that standing up for yourself and for your beliefs is *not* taking the easy route. My conclusion to it all was, "It's complicated."

The social unrest firmed up the youth and others to question the motives of the establishment, a.k.a. the government. Cultural mind-sets were being tweaked to focus on human rights, which we, the next in line to lead the world and to make our mark, thought was the next level in the evolvement of mankind. I could still imagine a peaceful world, and I was thankful that strong statements were being made by people who were much braver than me. Not knowing what else to do about the turmoil, I went out and bought a peace sign to wear around my neck. It was my statement, my way.

Chapter 13
Too Cool

"When they see me walkin' down the street, hey hey
When the fellas want to speak, hey hey
On their faces they wear silly smirks, 'cuz they know
I'm the king of the cool jerk
Cool jerk!"
—Sung by *The Capitols*, 1966

THERE REALLY WASN'T MUCH CALL for preschools or daycare centers in my neighborhood. Very few mothers worked outside of the home once they had children. If they did, usually another family member, grandmother or aunt, would be there to help out. It just wasn't common place, or necessary, to have someone else being involved with raising your children.

That's also why mothers couldn't wait until their kids could go to kindergarten. Even if you were only four years old, and your birthday fell right on the deadline of being able to get into kindergarten, you were going.

Most of the kids made it through elementary school okay, some being held back a couple of years down the road in first or second grade, but kindergarten itself was a piece of cake. Mostly it was time to socialize with your friends and a bit of learning the alphabet and numbers thrown in. There was a half a day of school during which was playtime, recess, naptime, snack time, learning to not hit anyone, getting the hang of standing in line single file, getting the hang of raising your hand to go to the restroom, and then getting on the bus to go home. This school thing was getting off on the right foot.

Just when you started to think that school was a fun place to go, you go into first grade. The teachers get serious and begin making you learn spelling, math, and how to read. We also learned about tests—the dreaded tests. Being the firstborn child, the *perfectionist*, I always wanted to get every answer correct. It is still etched into my memory, a certain test in first grade, when there appeared a question on a test: "A bird: (a) walks (b) hops (c) runs (d) jumps. This was a difficult question, and I racked my brain thinking about the birds in my neighborhood. Did they walk? Did they hop? Did they run? I didn't think they jumped. Deep breath. I could remember them walking. Yes, (a) walk. But when the teacher corrected the papers, mine came back with the wrong answer. The correct answer was (b) hop. Since I distinctly remember seeing birds walk I decided to challenge the teacher on this one. Bravely, and feeling justified, I walked up to the teacher's desk and told her that birds can walk. She looked down at me, pushed her glasses down her nose, and matter-of-factly said, "Birds hop." End of discussion. I had a minus 1 on this test and there was no more recourse. Even today, I look out my window occasionally and watch birds run and walk and hop, maybe even jump once in a while. Life teaches lessons, even in first grade, and this one fell under the categories of: "Life is never fair, never will be, and teachers are always right whether you like it or not."

My school experiences began at Pattengill Elementary School for kindergarten and first grade. Riding a bus was a lot of responsibility. You had to make sure you were on the right bus, try to sit by someone you liked, behave yourself along the way, and know when to get off. That's quite something for a five-year-old. So it was not surprising to me when I inadvertently forgot my winter coat and snow pants at school on a January day. With everything else I had to deal with at school, it didn't even occur to me that this was something out of the ordinary. Well, the look on my mom's face told it all. You would have thought that the world was coming to an end when I walked up the driveway in the midst of winter with no coat on. Mothers! They only worry about the small stuff, like coats and stuff, not even knowing what *we* have to go through every day. Mom told that story over and over throughout the years as if it was beyond belief. All I could think was, *Does she really have to tell everyone?*

During my first-grade year, our Cranbrook subdivision learned that we were getting a new school just for our neighborhood. A brand-spanking-new elementary school! With ninety kids just on our immediate block, with seven other streets and another neighborhood beyond, our bursting-at-the-seams baby boomer generation needed to be accommodated. It worked out well for us. Now we could walk to school every day. We walked, ran, jump roped, and ice skated the half mile to school in the morning, home again for lunch, back to school, and then at 3:15 p.m. we were free.

For my first semester of second grade, John Allen Elementary School wasn't yet completed, so we rode a bus to Pittsfield School where we infiltrated a different neighborhood, and were treated somewhat like "squatters" for a semester. Just knowing that we were going to have our own modern, state-of-the art school in a few months made it all worthwhile.

So far in my history, the academic world, it seemed, had treated me kindly. My teachers were kind, nonthreatening, and didn't seem to force the issue of growing up too fast. Second grade became our Waterloo. Mrs. Winklehaus took no hostages. She was ready to conquer and defeat any baby-like tendencies we had left. Crying, whining, and excuses only infuriated her. Sit up tall, pull your chair in, eyes straight ahead at the blackboard, and no touching or talking with the kid next to you at any time. She was General Patton in drag. Dark hair pulled back in a bun, glasses, a grandmotherly dress, clompy black shoes, a face that didn't crack a smile much, and on top of that, a voice that made chills run up and down your spine. I excelled in second grade out of fear.

If Mrs. Winklehaus said that your lunch must be eaten before you may go out on the playground, you better believe there was nothing left in my Lennon Sisters metal lunch box before I got up from the table. If Mrs. Winklehaus said that we must learn three verses of "O' Little Town of Bethlehem" before the Christmas concert date, you know that we learned them backward and forward and that our parents would be very impressed. For some reason, my mother loved Mrs. Winklehaus. It must have been out of respect.

Not all of my classmates were as submissive as I was. The one boy who dared to buck Mrs. Winklehaus was a brave soul. He stood his ground, and I admired his tenacity, but Johnny had a miserable second-grade experience. In today's world, he would have been labeled with ADD or some other diagnosis, but in this era there were no excuses for disrespectful behavior, especially in Mrs. Winklehaus's world. The other kids in the classroom would sit in awe, mouths wide open, watching and cringing as Johnny talked back, mocked, and entirely disobeyed the general. He was placed at a table, not a desk, in the back of the room, so he wouldn't disrupt the others. But that only made Johnny try harder to get the goat of our teacher. When the second semester began, and we began life in our new John Allen Elementary School, Johnny did not return to our class. I don't know if he moved away, or if he had won or lost the battle, but the war of wits ended. The angelic, well-behaved, obedient children did their time for the remainder of the school year.

We had cement to play Four Square on, a terraced grassy hill to do somersaults down, a giant oak tree to sit under, and a spacious open area with playground equipment; all of it was the recess area we explored. As it goes though, in elementary school, just as important as book learning is also learning your place in the social structure. You could call it social survival. We avoided the bullies, learned who the leaders were, admired the athletes, and found out who was nice and who wasn't. We discovered the pecking order and our place within it. We learned how to make friends and the hard lesson of how to keep them as friends. We challenged ourselves to go as high as we could on the swings, and jumping off, learning the very important lesson of falling flat on our faces and getting up acting as if nothing happened at all. We found out about our physical abilities playing King of the Hill where the strongest and fastest person wins, and that person usually isn't you, but when it comes to writing an essay, or turning homework in on time, you do really well. Multitudes of lessons are learned getting "down and dirty" on the playground, and most of those lessons stick with us for a lifetime.

Other lessons learned include what you might call "testing the limits." After a fifth-grade gym class one afternoon, a few of us girls decided it would be "fun" to hide in the girl's locker room after school let out for the day. Our semi-well-thought-out plan was to go into the locker room and hide out until everyone had vacated the building, and when the coast was clear, we could have free reign of the school. It would be a blast to run up and down the halls screaming and being wild and crazy girls. So, as we gathered up our books and left the classroom, we nonchalantly ditched into the girl's locker room. Our excitement built as we realized our daring and defiance. Then, at the other end of the locker room, we heard a door open. Our quick strategy was to go into the toilet stalls and stand on the toilet seats and be really quiet. I am quite sure that we weren't as quiet as we imagined we were, and Miss Parker, the school secretary, said, "What are you girls doing in here?" With saucer-shaped eyes and guilty faces, off we went to the principal's office. The question of "What were you girls doing in the locker room after school hours?" was presented again by Mr. Nichols. Some "I don't knows" floated out of our mouths, and with phone calls to our parents, we were sent home to face the firing squad of questions from our dads and moms. Feigning innocence I told my parents that it wasn't *my* idea, and I really didn't know *what* those girls were up to. Separating yourself from the "bad guys" was always the way to go. "You better never do that again!" they said. "Don't worry. I won't!" I said.

Elementary school is where you learn the life lessons that stay with you forever—the hard lesson of one day being on top of the world and being the coolest kid in your class, and then the next day you feel like you're being treated like the biggest jerk who ever walked the earth. The ups and downs that come your way, trying to figure it all out, striving to keep a balance, and not taking life too seriously is a lot of responsibility for a kid.

Chapter 14
No Sniveling

"Tradin' my time for the pay I get, Livin' on money
that I ain't made yet
Gotta keep goin', gotta get make my way, While I
live for the end of the day
Yeah, yeah! 'Cause it's a five o'clock world..."
—Sung by *The Vogues, 1965*

AS THE YEARS TRANSITIONED FROM the carefree and protected childhood days into an adolescence that bore expectations, it was becoming obvious to me that living a life with few responsibilities was not in the cards. As a gathering of girls, Diane, Susie, Betsy, and I decided that we were going to announce to the world, a.k.a. our neighborhood, that we were ready, willing, and able to *babysit* other people's kids, who weren't exactly *babies,* but that's a whole other topic.

Yes, we thought, eleven years old is the perfect age to begin offering our babysitting services. We made flyers with our names and phone numbers and put them in the neighbor's mailboxes that were attached to the house right next to their front doors. With all of the children in the neighborhood we felt certain that our phones would be ringing right off the hook.

After we delivered the flyers, then we told our mothers of our idea. If our moms didn't agree with our new venture, well, the flyers were out there already so how could they argue with the demand that we will surely create? It was the "do it first, then ask forgiveness" rule of thumb. My mom seemed fine with the job search, although she thought that twelve years old would be a better age to start. Such was the start of my working career.

A few months later the neighborhood mothers began asking my mom if I could babysit. At thirty-five cents an hour, and with no negotiations, I was in demand on most weekends and even more days in the summertime. The year I was thirteen I had an almost full-time summer job watching Jeff, Jeri, and Jay. That was the year the notion called *responsibility* made quite an impression on me. With three children under my care, watching them constantly, feeding them, and keeping them entertained for the entire day, it helped me understand what a huge undertaking it was to have children. Jeff, the oldest, was a diabetic. He was six years old and already knew how to give himself his insulin shot. I was very glad for that, but, as his mom said, "You will need to know what to do if Jeff has an 'episode.'" I really didn't know what an episode was, or how to detect whether he was having one. What I do know is that I was always on the lookout for an "episode." I was told that if Jeff had one that I should make him drink some orange juice and he would probably be okay, but if he went into a coma he could die. For a thirteen-year-old, that felt like a huge responsibility.

Jeff never had an episode on my watch. I made sure that he ate meals on time and had healthy snacks during the afternoon. We kept busy playing games inside and outdoors. The board game Operation was our favorite. Jeri Lynn, the four-year-old, loved watching *Mr. Rogers' Neighborhood* and *Mr. Dress Up* on TV. She was the cutest little girl, and I nicknamed her "Monkey" because she loved jumping up into my arms. Little Jay was the youngest at three years old and followed us goodheartedly in whatever we were doing.

That summer was a stepping-stone from being a child to learning about maturity. My friends weren't relating to my new attitude. While they were climbing fences and riding bikes, I was beginning the training of adulthood. What we all learned eventually, whether it was mowing lawns, helping with your dad's business, or babysitting, was that having a job was your ticket to freedom. Money in your pocket gave you purchasing power. After getting paying jobs, the purchases of choice in our neighborhood were: record albums, five-speed banana-seat bikes, mini-bikes, go-carts, electric guitars, Beatles wigs—yes, Beatles wigs—Beatle magazines, and skateboards.

I began to buy my own clothes. No longer did I have to wear the JCPenney catalogue outfits ordered by my mom. I could go to Jacobson's and other designer boutiques down on campus. I loved picking out my own preppy clothes, or paisley shorts with a bright orange tee shirt. When I bought a blue nylon University of Michigan shirt at Moe Sport Shop with the large maize-colored "M" on it, I was the envy of the entire neighborhood. It was so very groovy! This had to be the beginning of the team-sponsored athletic wear craze that has made these institutions plenty of pocket change over the years. My brother bought the shirt from me for $10 because it was absolutely the coolest.

Another item we could buy with our own money was smokes. Cigarettes were definitely a rite of passage to adulthood. Of course our parents had to be the last to know we had cigarettes in our possession, and sneaking around made it all the more fun. As I was doing homework in my bedroom one evening, my dad walked in my room and there on my desk sat my purse, wide open, with a pack of Marlboro filters. "What are you doing with these?" he asked.

"Oh, those?" I stammered. "Those belong to, ah, my friend, ah, Mary."

Looking very serious, he asked, "Do you smoke?"

"No," I said. "Mary wanted me to hold them for her." I added, "I know smoking is bad for you."

"Okay," he said as he walked away, never mentioning it again.

At the time, I felt *somewhat* justified with the "white lie" I told my dad. I didn't really enjoy smoking, but it was just really hip to have cigarettes in my purse. If you were sitting in a restaurant with your friends, and they decided to have a smoke, it was so grown up to pull out your own pack and light one up.

It was delightful to be part of the crowd, and at this age peer pressure was intense, and directed pretty much everything that I did or could get away with.

The summer between eighth and ninth grades, just before school was let out, my mother informed me that I was going to work full time for Dog 'n' Suds. I didn't seem to have a choice in the matter. I tried to ask why I had to work full time, but to no avail; that was just the way it was going to be. Mom and the neighbor lady, Mrs. Rose, worked there during the school year, but they wanted the summer off so they could hang out at the Rose's pool. I suppose they were going to do other things too, like take care of their children, etc., but it sure seemed like a railroad job to me. So, hence, I began a short career as a waitress.

Dog 'n' Suds had a horseshoe-shaped dining counter and a full dining room for table seating. It also had drive-up service and a waitress would come out to your car and take your order. Then the driver would roll the driver's window up just a couple of inches so the waitress could hook a tray onto the window. The trays had removable rubber mesh mats on them to hold the root beer mugs above the slopped, wet soda pop that was spilled when the waitress carried your food order out to the car. It kept the coney dogs and Texas twinburgers above the wetness also. At the horseshoe counter, working men gathered around watching Mrs. Corwin make fresh donuts topped with chocolate or vanilla frosting. She would bring the donuts up from the boiling grease, top them with the frosting and add coconut or peanuts to some of them. Eating them as soon as you could touch them without burning your fingers was the greatest treat of all. No frosting was necessary when they were warm and slightly crispy. I thought Mrs. Corwin made the best donuts in the world. Her son, Bud, was the owner. He was a big, gruff, sort of man, who meant business. He only hired people he liked, and I was certainly quite intimidated by him.

My brain was on overload learning all the intricacies of waiting on people, saying the right things to them, making milkshakes and malteds (and knowing the difference), drawing the root beer with just the right amount of foam, washing the root beer mugs, getting food to customers while it was still warm, and counting the correct change on the "push the number key down" cash register that did not tell you how much the change back to the customer would be. I had to figure that out in my head. I fumbled my way through the first summer with the help of the other waitresses. The working men enjoyed the entertainment and didn't hesitate to make their joking remarks. They seemed to get a kick out of teasing a fourteen-year-old to the verge of tears, or at least embarrassment.

The state police officer who ate breakfast at Dog 'n' Suds every week day had very high expectations, and he surely let me know what those were. Two dollops of heavy cream in his coffee, eggs sunny-side up and lightly basted, and his toast better still be warm. Two years later when I had my driving test to get my license, this officer was my test official. I was petrified. I believe my mother was the instigator of making sure he was the officer I tested with. For some strange reason, my parents did not really want me to get my driver's license. Possibly, just maybe, it was because I had always been a little ditsy, forgetful, and absent-minded as a child, and they couldn't quite imagine me behind the wheel of a car and responsible for my life and the lives of others. Maybe mother's motive was valid. If I could pass the driving test with this ornery, no-nonsense state police officer, then I may possibly have my parents' blessing to drive. I prayed that he would not make me parallel park. I prayed I would not act too nervous. I prayed that I wouldn't hit anything during the test. Fortunately, no parallel parking, no major mistakes, and I kept my cool. I passed.

At this age, my goal was to strive for independence and the ability to make my own decisions. This really meant trying to figure out which crowd of friends to hang out with and what roads to go down, or what path not to take. Choices were becoming much more critical and important to the person I would be.

The workplace can teach responsibility and accountability. It also gives you the almighty paycheck as an incentive to develop maturity. Obtaining the paycheck gives you the freedom to be who you are and not be beholden to another. By this, I mean, that you have the freedom to make more choices for yourself without the restraint that others may put on you if you are dependent upon them. This may sound selfish, but it is the opposite of selfish. It is actually the greatest freedom of all.

Chapter 15
Dog Days

"Hot town, summer in the city
Back of my neck getting dirty and gritty
Been down, isn't it a pity
Doesn't seem to be a shadow in the city
All around, people looking half dead
Walking on the sidewalk, hotter than a match head."
—Sung by *The Lovin' Spoonful, 1966*

ON A SWELTERING HOT AUGUST day, the world seems to stand still. Even the blades of the lawn grass seem to stand still to avoid any exertion in the heat of the day. Asphalt streets become sizzling griddles, and the air feels like you're standing in front of a fiery coal furnace that you cannot seem to walk away from.

The few respites are lying on a cool lawn, running through the oscillating sprinkler, and eating Popsicles. Window fans were the common cooling unit in our Cranbrook homes, and standing in front of one for a few minutes was like heaven. Some homes had an air conditioner installed in a window, which might cool down one room of the house, but having air conditioning that cooled the entire house was not known to society yet. On the evening news, the announcers would give the total number of deaths related to the "heat wave." Usually it was elderly people in larger cities who had succumbed to the stifling hot weather from heat stroke. So, finding ways to survive the extreme temperature was the task of the day.

On one such sultry August day, we were sitting on the Bell's log fence swapping stories and telling tales when a quick summer thunderstorm popped up. The rain came down in vertical sheets of water that seemed to chase each other down the street. The downpour that immediately drenched us instantly cooled our warm skin, and we began running wildly around the lawn being energized by the downpour. The street gutters and sewers couldn't keep up with the deluge from the skies, and it created a torrential river that flowed down Cranbrook Road. In our minds, nothing better could have happened that day! We were laughing and splashing and letting the force of the water flow past our legs as it coursed its way toward the sewer grates. Just as we were having the time of our lives pushing through the knee-deep water and challenging each other to who could stand up the longest at the sewer grate where the water was the most volatile, our mothers began to poke their heads out of the doors and call us to come inside. We begged them to allow us to stay out and play in the heavy rain. Most of the mothers let us continue our fun since we were already wet and there wasn't very much lightning with the storm. It was a phenomenal time that we could embrace this act of nature up close and personal, sensing the force it could create within a moment's time. When the rain started to let up, we finally dragged our tired and wet bodies into the nice warm comfort of our homes. Exhilarated and still reveling in our adventure of the day, I realized how insignificant humans can be to go up against the power that nature holds—the mighty force of a waterfall, the strength of a stiff wind pushing against your body, the brightness of the big, yellow sun that commands your eyes to squint. Nature lets you know that you are not the master, only a subject of its glory. But then, just when we feel this diminutiveness, we realize our connection to it all! We *are* an integral, working part of a huge organism, the planet Earth itself.

As a summer ramps up, the heat seems to put smiles on faces and can even relax the attitudes of the grouchiest adults. This meant that parents said yes a whole lot more than normal. That was one of the reasons why summer was so great! The Mikkelsens were a fairly cool family in our neighborhood. What made them cool? Well, they had a lot kids in the family to goof off with, and we didn't feel much adult pressure at their house. Dr. Mikkelsen gave his kids their vaccination shots at home, he left his pocket change on his dresser that we would use for the ice cream man, and I could go on and on. But what really made them cool was that they belonged to the Chippewa Swim Club. And what made them even cooler was that they owned a red 1967 Pontiac

Firebird convertible. So when one day Dr. Mikkelsen said that he would take as many kids as could fit into the convertible to the swim club we were *all* feeling pretty cool. We ran to our houses to get our bathing suits and towels and to tell our moms that we were heading out to the swim club with the Mikkelsens. We jam packed as many kids as we could squeeze in, with Johnny Mikkelsen and David Bell sitting on the back trunk with their legs hanging into the back seat. Everyone else was sitting on laps and squished together. Dr. Mikkelsen turned up the volume on the car's radio and away we flew down the road singing "A Little Bit o' Soul" at the top of our lungs. We hollered for him to go faster, but I do think that he may have been a little nervous to get stopped by officers with so many people in the car.

I Think it Is So Groovy Now That People Are Finally Gettin' Together...

For a few years, in the summertime, Cranbrook Road held a block party. We closed off a section of the street for a night, ate lots of great food, played music, danced, and got to be wild and crazy kids. It was the only time I remember seeing my dad in a pair of matching plaid shorts Mom had gotten both of them for this special occasion. I remember him grumbling about wearing them, but he did. Just once, for Mom.

From their perch on the picnic tables in the middle of the street, our parents watched as the young ones danced the Pony, the Freddie, and the Swim. Some of the grownups were brave enough to try some of the dances, imitating us mostly in a mocking way, and then they settled into their comfort zone and began doing the Twist. It was one of the few times that the two generations tried to come to some common ground and succeeded.

Another common ground was neighborhood projects. I am not quite sure what summer it was, because memory would have it that all summers seemed to stream together, but it was the year that my dad, a jack-of-all-trades, and a master at most of them, decided that a one-stall garage with a tool bench on one side would be just right for our needs. He took a few weeks off from work to devote to the major undertaking. After the cement was poured and the walls were raised, the neighborhood boys became curious about the building project happening in our driveway and, with the guidance of Dad and Mr. Rose, started swinging hammers along with them. Every morning David Bell would sit on our back porch waiting for my dad to exit and get started for the day. As the morning progressed, more boys would join them and the carpentry class began. Many a bent nail was thrown into a bucket, but Dad and Mr. Rose persevered with patience. When it got to the point for the roof to be shingled, Dad came up with the idea that it would go a lot faster if all of the kids in the neighborhood helped him. It had been a hot day so Dad and Mr. Rose decided we should do this roofing after the sun was lower in the sky. The word got around the block that day, and by 6:00 that night we had about ten kids on top of the roof of the garage ready and willing to nail some shingles down. Of course we had no idea what we were doing, but somehow we were organized into a smooth-running assembly line with Dad and Mr. Rose giving orders. My job was to hand out nails to the boys with the hammers. I made the boys let me pound a few nails, and then I was just fine with being the "nail pail girl." A few hours into the project I stood back in amazement at the progress we were making and how well everyone was working together. The neighborhood boys were proud of being included in "men's work" and took pride in what they were doing. I thought it should be my duty to make some Kool-Aid for everyone—since it was my house and they were all working for us. So, into the house I went with no clue as to how to make it. I read the directions on the little package of powder and decided to improvise by adding 50 percent more sugar to the recipe. My Kool-Aid was a hit! I went down in Cranbrook history as the best Kool-Aid barista around. I took glasses of the syrupy liquid up the ladder to the "men at work" and they slurped it down with gusto. They not only had adrenaline running through their veins but now had the best sugar high you can imagine. We worked into the night with spotlights rigged up on the roof and a transistor radio blasting out "Wooly Bully" and "Mony, Mony." We sang along to all the popular songs in scratchy harmony until we finally finished up around midnight. As we climbed down the ladder for the last time, the Cranbrook kids felt as if we had achieved a job well done.

Going to bed that night, I remember sensing the secure warmth of the neighborhood surrounding me. I lay quietly letting what we had just accomplished soak in, and drifting off to sleep, I knew that this night would create a bond for all involved.

The next morning, as my dad was able to get a real look at the roofing job in the daylight, he said in his critical builder voice, "Not too bad, not too bad at all."

Chapter 16
Essence of Existence

"On my honor I will try to do my duty to God and my country, to help other people at all times and to obey the Girl Scout law."
—The Girl Scout Promise, 1960s
—Written by Juliette Gordon Low, Founder of Girl Scouts of America

OUR PARENTS SURVIVED A NINE-YEAR Great Depression and a World War that lasted another six years of their lives. Getting through those challenges was no small feat. This experience also made lasting impressions upon them, but in the end, they acquired the confidence that our government could pull them out of any bad situation that came along. After World War II ended, the United States ruled the world and its citizens lived in the most respected, kind, and safe place in the world. As kids, we knew this to be true because our parents were very proud of winning the Great War, proud of our booming economy, proud of providing better lives for their children, and proud of the American flag.

On each and every Memorial Day and the Fourth of July, we were packed into our sky blue-and-white Pontiac and then off to Ypsilanti and Grammie's house we went. The Memorial Day Parade came down Michigan Avenue and turned onto River Street passing in front of Grammie's and ended a little way down the street at the Highland Cemetery. Because this was the day that you "decorated" the graves of soldiers, Grammie called this "Decoration Day." That is what Memorial Day was called when it began as a holiday to honor those who died in the Civil War. As the parade marched by, bands played patriotic songs and World War Veterans wearing their uniforms proudly marched carrying the Stars and Stripes. Standing along the parade route, the fathers and grandfathers, who had also served their country, saluted them as they passed. They had a common bond, a band of brothers, giving an acknowledgment of gratitude for actively preserving our freedom.

On the Fourth of July, the parade came down Michigan Avenue all the way through downtown Ypsilanti. Michigan Avenue was only three houses away from Grammie's house, so we walked down to the corner and stood by the Dairy Queen to watch the parade. Grammie had fifty-four great-grandchildren and many of them came to her house on the Fourth of July to watch the parade because it was a very special day for us. It was the special day we all got a nickel from Grammie to buy the smallest ice cream cone that Dairy Queen had, the "kiddie cone"! She saved nickels all year long, and on that day she put a nickel in the palm of every great-grandchild who showed up for the parade. Grammie wasn't one to part with her money at any whim—let's just say she was frugal—so, not only was this fun, it meant a lot to all of us. It was fun for Grammie also, and you could see the sparkle in her eyes as she watched us run down the street to the Dairy Queen.

After the parade, we hugged Great-Grammie good-bye and headed home for the second treat of the day, the fireworks! Our house was two blocks away from Buhr Park, which had the best fireworks for miles around. The front yard would be full of relatives and friends, our blankets spread out on the lawn, and then the sparklers would be passed out. Drawing our names with the lighted sticks, running through the grass and creating streaks of light across the dimming evening sky, we felt the excitement of the night, waiting for the best part yet to come. Then, as the first big boom sounded, and the test firework was shot up into the sky, we settled onto our blankets, and thus began the "oohs and aahs" that happen all across the United States on the Fourth of July. The display of fireworks seemed to get better with every year we lived in the house, and as we lay on our backs and looked up into the night sky, we savored every special burst of light. We moaned our remorse after the booming "grand finale" lit up the sky with all its glory and trudged our way to bed still smelling the lingering firework smoke in the air. The next day we would run over to Buhr Park and try to find shrapnel from the fireworks. Sometimes we would find a piece or two of burnt, heavy paper, but amazingly most of it disappeared to somewhere we never figured out.

There were only a few times I remember being able to watch television in school. The first time was when Alan Shepard, the very first American to travel into space, was launched by a rocket that took his Freedom 7 capsule into the altitudes for fifteen minutes. It was a successful mission that ended with Shepard landing in the Atlantic Ocean safe and sound. The second time was when President John F. Kennedy declared that the Cuban Missile Crisis was over. It had been a thirteen-day standoff with Cuba and the Soviet Union over nuclear missiles that were being stationed off of Cuba. Soviet nuclear weapons so close to the United States was making Americans a little uncomfortable. President Kennedy decided to surround Cuba with navy ships and submarines to let them know that we were not going to put up with it. Being that the Soviet Union had nuclear weapons, things got a little tense here in the United States of America. But there was President Kennedy on TV telling us that we had come to some agreements, the standoff was over, and there would be no nuclear weapons in Cuba.

A breath in, and a breath out. Good, there will not be a war. The Cold War still existed, though, and America thought that with a push of a button, we could all be annihilated. It didn't consume me, but, just in case the unimaginable did happen, I had a game plan. *Let's just say,* I thought, *I happen to be walking home from school someday, and, out of the blue, I notice a mushroom-*

shaped cloud in the sky that was formed from an atomic blast. I will run to the neighbors on Towner Boulevard who have a bomb shelter in their backyard. Nonchalantly, no, actually desperately, I will ask the owners if they mind me crawling in with them. How could they possibly say no? Perfect scenario.

Survival

I needed to know how to survive. I was a captive audience and an enthusiastic apprentice in Girl Scout Troop 594. We began as Brownies in second grade and continued on through seventh grade as Cadets. The entire six years, Mrs. Kiddon was our leader. She led with an iron-fisted determination to make us into the best Girl Scout Troop in Michigan. There were absolutely no excuses in her book. We feared, and I really mean to say, respected, Mrs. Kiddon. She may have led with no nonsense, but she made it up with all of the great adventures she took us on. The badges we could acquire ran the gamut from knitting and childcare to weaving, woodworking, and camping. You could be as domestic or as adventurous as you wanted when earning badges, but when Mrs. Kiddon took us camping, you had better buck up. There were no pantywaists allowed.

We weeded out the froufrou girls around third grade, and then Mrs. Kiddon was on a roll. Camp Hilltop, Camp Mill Lake, Camp Linden, and Camp Sugarloaf Lake, we tackled them all. We learned how to cook campfire stew, which was ground beef and canned vegetable soup mixed together over the campfire. We made our "sit-a-pons" out of two squares of oil cloth sewn together and stuffed with rags to sit "upon" by the campfire at night, or whenever we were allowed to take a break. To wash dishes we took nylon netting and sewed in a drawstring at the top and made a "swishee bag" to put our dirty dishes in. Then you just swish the bag through the dish soap water, then through the rinse water, hang it on the clothesline and you're done!

Most of the time we had a choice about what badges we wanted to earn, but the one badge Mrs. Kiddon wanted all of us to get was the camping badge that required sleeping outside all night under the stars. Bravely, we laid down our dew cloths, which were oil cloth tablecloths on the ground, unfolded our sleeping bags, crawled in, and looked up at the stars in the night sky. I slept pretty well that night, dreaming of wild bears that were looking for some sweet, tender morsels to munch on. The bears would find us young, innocent, slightly dirty, sweet girls and say, "These little snacks will do just fine!" Yes, I knew my mom and dad would miss me, but they would be proud and take comfort in knowing that I valiantly tried to earn my Girl Scout camping badge.

I don't know how many times a year our Girl Scout troop went camping, but it seemed like at least once a month we were on some sort of excursion. In the winter months, we would go to Mill Lake and slide down the hill from the lodge or look for tracks of animals in the snow and try to figure out what animal could have possibly made that. In the summertime, we went to Cedar Lake for two weeks. Two glorious weeks of s'mores at night and pancakes in the morning, pine trees and water, with all with the Girl Scout morals thrown in. The high emotions were running between feeling mature and independent, to feeling separation and homesickness, but between the leather crafts, earning your swimming badge, and all the other activities the leaders had planned, there wasn't much time for feeling sorry for yourself. One girl in my cabin tried so hard to get sent home by crying and sobbing relentlessly. It didn't work. The counselors just explained to her that she was not going home. No way, no how. She finally decided that she had better start enjoying herself or this was not going to be much fun. We all rallied around her and soon she became a part of our "cabin family."

Grammie wrote me a letter while I was at Cedar Lake Camp. It was written on a greeting card she herself had received. She cut off their names, pasted it to a paper doily, and wrote how much she missed me. My homesickness flowed, and tears ran down my cheeks as I read it. In Grammie's world there had been no Girl Scouts, no camping. For her, everyday life had been hard enough. She had told the story of her father sending her down to the logger's camp in Williamsport, Pennsylvania, where she grew up, to get a job cooking for the lumbermen. She came home to her father after talking with the logging men and told him that she would be making $1.00 per week. Her "pop" told her to tell them that she would be making $1.50 per week. His rationale was this: A good pair of shoes cost at least $1.50, and you should be able to at least buy a pair of good shoes for a week's work. Life for Grammie had been farming chores, cooking, cleaning, and taking care of young ones. How could she even relate to going to a Girl Scout camp? I am sure she couldn't, but she cared enough to know that two weeks was a long time to be away from family and that I would love to hear from her. I did.

Our friends, the Roses, belonged to a private inland lake. On hot Sunday afternoons, our family would be invited to join them for a picnic, swimming, and boating at Independence Lake. After about a forty-five-minute car ride we arrived at the lake. The kids rushed to the edge of the water and waded through the silvery minnows and marshy grasses to get to the open water, and then we could really goof off. The boys would dive underwater and then sneak over to grab the girls' legs to scare the heck out of them. Girls screaming, boys laughing, we sure knew how to entertain ourselves. Physical activity meant veracious appetites. A hotdog, some chips, and a few Oreo cookies on the side, and we were ready to run back into the water. "Oh no!" the mothers would holler after us. "You cannot go into the water for a half an hour after you eat!" And then they followed it up with, "You will get leg cramps and drown!" A half an hour felt like two hours. So we chased chipmunks or played catch with Frisbees until we had the affirmation from our moms that it was safe now, and rest assured, we would not drown from having leg cramps so bad that we would be motionless and unable to swim to shore.

Dad and Mr. Rose would take us tent camping at Independence Lake also. Our water supply was a hand pump that required, first, we went down to the lake and got a bucket of water and "primed" the pump by dumping the lake water into a place in the pump, which would create suction as we pumped the handle of the pump. The suction pulled the well water up, and finally good, fresh, water came flooding out of the pump. We learned to water ski behind the Roses' boat. The boys seemed to be better at it because they had stronger upper bodies, or maybe they had a better sense of how to leverage themselves to get up, but Mr. Rose was patient and let us try over and over until we got it. Perpetually sunburned noses, freckled faces, and stubbed toes were the fashion statement of the day.

Up North

Going "up north" in Michigan meant going anywhere north of Lansing, Michigan. Usually about once a summer, Nonnie and Orville would take me and Mark up north with them to go fishing or to see their old stomping grounds or to just be "fudgies," as the tourists are called up there. Loving the carefree and never-stop-moving lifestyle, it seemed as though Nonnie and Orville had been in every city, village, and burg in the Upper and Lower Peninsula of Michigan, most of Pennsylvania, and Florida. On any given trip with Nonnie, when the clock struck 3:00, Nonnie would say, "Orville, there is a place we can stop up the road a couple of miles." The "place" was always what you might classify as a "dive bar," meaning it usually was a questionable tavern of sorts. *Not* stopping was never an option. Nonnie's daily routine during the entire lifetime that I knew her was that at 4:00 every afternoon, she had two "shells" (as she called them) of draft beer. It didn't have to be a special brand or kind of beer, it just had to be *beer*. Even when she was at home, she had her certain bars that she would frequent. It was her social hour, and during her normal routine, she usually didn't share this part of her life with Orville. Orville stayed home, sharing his solitude with his whiskey and 7-Up.

One such time, we were driving north on M-123 in the Upper Peninsula. Nonnie piped up and told us about a log cabin bar on the corner of M-123 and Highway 28, "Just up and over the hill," she said. As we walked in, Orville said to Mark and me, "Come over here and look at this." He walked us past the bar and to the pine log wall and began to tell us the story of a night he was in this tavern, sitting at the bar, talking with the locals, and a woman came in and shot at her husband with a rifle because he had overstayed his allotted time at the bar. The bullet missed the husband, maybe intentionally, and was buried into the wood. It was still there! Mark and I endured Nonnie's two draft beer "moments" with our own kiddie cocktails and French fries, or some sort of deep fried food. We would have the freedom to explore the bar or the territory outside, just checking in once in a while to let Nonnie and Orville know we were still alive.

After the two beers, it was time to figure out where we were going to stay the night. Reservations were never made, so we had the ritual of finding a place where Nonnie could stay. Her criteria were: a clean room according to her standards, a TV, and a firm meticulous bed. The ritual went like this: We would pull up to some cute cabins or a motel where all the rooms were connected in a long row, and Nonnie would walk into the office. Orville stayed in the car to avoid embarrassment. I went in with her a couple of times and then I understood why Orville stayed in the car. She always asked to see the room. As the manager or owner led her in, she carefully eyed it over, went to the bed and pulled back the sheets to see if the mattress, sheets, and bedspread were clean, she felt the mattress to see if it was firm enough for her, then opened closets and drawers, checking for dirt. All the while, the owner was watching her dissect the entire room. Nonnie was not afraid to make comments if it didn't look up to her standards. Everyone got an earful and then she would state that we would need to find another place. We always hoped that the first place we stopped would be good enough for her, but it usually wasn't. Orville would grumble a little, and I would say, "Nonnie, this place looks just fine!" Nonnie would reply, "I cannot sleep on that dirty mattress!" Or "The closet had dirt swept into it!" Then off we went to the next place up the road. Sometimes though, there were not a lot of choices and Nonnie had to settle with what was available. When that happened, she would voice her complaints to the management and to us. That's when Orville would take us all to dinner and get Nonnie another beer.

Going up North meant going back in time. Pine forests and two-lane roads would wind into a small village that usually had a diner, a motel, a gas station, and maybe a convenience store. There were no franchises of any sort. Businesses were all locally owned and ran by people who lived there their entire lives. We stopped in Pinconning for cheese, Standish for pepperoni sticks, and on Highway 2 for the best pasties in the UP. There was smoked whitefish in Paradise, and the huge cinnamon rolls in McMillan would feed four people. The souvenir shops were the highlight of the North Country. Indian beaded necklaces and painted tomahawks for the kids, wooden drums that had rubber laced to the top instead of leather, and there was always a table of items made out of cedar wood. Cedar jewelry boxes, woodland pictures that were glued onto a cedar plaque, shining bright with varnish, and cedar peace pipes with dyed chicken feathers dangling on a sting of rawhide—now these were treasures you could not find anyplace else. Mark and I could spend hours trying to decide between a sling shot or a cap gun. I wanted the Indian dolls with the leather clothing, both the squaw and the warrior, but Orville would round us up to get on the road again.

Driving up Old US 23, there was an area where stands of white birch trees were plentiful. I had always lived in the Ann Arbor area. I had never, ever seen birch trees before, and I could not get enough of them. I asked Orville if we could stop and get some birch bark from a tree. Nonnie kept saying that it was illegal to take bark from the trees, but Orville pulled the car over anyway. With a pocket knife he let us peel some bark off and keep it for a memento. The natural souvenirs were the best! Nonnie couldn't give us too much resistance in taking our treasures from the earth. On every trip to the North, Nonnie had a habit of digging up at least one little tree, birch or pine, and placing it in a Dixie cup to plant when she returned home. Her backyard was full of trees that had survived the Dixie cup.

As you traveled "up North" you could sense the Great Spirit of the Indians. You could imagine their lives in the woods and on the waters, living in the wigwams and traveling the rivers in birch bark canoes. I would try to walk softly through the woods, not making any twig snap under my feet, as I was told the Indians did to sneak up on deer as they hunted.

I longed to be close to nature, strive to understand it, and learn to survive in it, and with it. If you can adapt to situations that will confront you in the natural environment, you gain the confidence to survive the situations that life itself can put in front of you as you go through this world. You learn that what Mother Earth gives us is what we need to survive.

"We need only listen to what the Earth is telling us."
—Thomas Berry, CP, Earth Scholar

Chapter 17
Can't Explain

"I'm not trying to cause a big sensation,
I'm just talkin' 'bout my generation."
—Sung by *The Who, 1965*

"So, why does your generation think they are so special?"
he asked. Those words not only surprised me but made me feel
embarrassed, guilty, and angry, all at the same time.

I was sitting comfortably in a circle of sofas and overstuffed
chairs with three editors asking me about why I thought I could
write a book about my generation. One guy was about forty-five
years old, being born in the later 1960s, the other male looked as
though he had been born in the later 1970s, and the beautiful,

perfectly manicured, young woman wasn't a day over twenty-five. And the question was presented.

The notion of being special had never crossed my mind. How could I possibly answer this question without sounding vain? "I think we lived in a period of time that was special," I said.

Leaving their office, I felt deflated and a bit stunned. I needed time to reflect on that question. I tried to view myself from the perspective of a person younger and from a different generation and tried to imagine how I would observe the "boomers" if I wasn't one of them. *Maybe we, the children of the '50s and '60s, do give ourselves too much credit for what we think we accomplished. Maybe we* do *have an elite attitude,* I wondered.

The mid-60s was a time in which idealism and philosophy became a very "in" thing. More and more of the youth were able to go to colleges and universities where deeper thinking and the nobility of principles were promoted. Because we were free to have utopian thoughts, it was our opinion that, yes, there was a chance for world peace, and in fact, our generation was going to make it happen. We felt summoned as youth to make the world a better place. Woman's lib, conservation of our natural resources, equality of the races, combating world hunger, world health organizations—all of these movements evolved from our "idealism" of what we thought could be fixed. If you strive to make the world a more peaceful planet, we thought, it will happen!

Giving the peace sign, with the index and second finger in a "V" formation, became our statement. The iconic symbol of our generation, the peace symbol, was being plastered everywhere. I remember kids stealing the hood ornaments off of Mercedes-

Benz cars because they *somewhat* looked like a peace symbol. (I suppose the act of stealing was not congruent with the ideal of peace, but that probably did not cross the minds of those doing it.) Our generation visualized ourselves as being free, being earthy, being mellow, being intelligent, and especially being the remedy for the world's ailments.

So, as I thought about it, maybe it's true. Maybe our generation has a high opinion of ourselves. I don't think we did that consciously with any sort of intent. It stemmed from the positive force we felt at that particular place in time and our abundant energy for change. As kids, we had known that our opportunities were endless. It began with our parents and their positive, forward momentum. The majority of those parents wanted the best for the next generation. They didn't fake it; they really believed in it. The limitless possibilities for their children were ready for the taking, and we, as a generation, grabbed it and ran. We ran so hard and so strong that our parents threw up their hands in mostly shock and disbelief of where we were taking this freedom. It was what we had to do.

As with any yin-yang, there is bad with the good. Our quest for a free lifestyle led many to experiment with mind-expanding drugs and sexual freedom, and to "push the envelope" to understanding everything they could about what this life has to offer. Some of the youth seemed to "check out," which meant they didn't want anything to do with the society of the day. The majority of the boomer generation, though, tempered their freedom quest with responsibility, most likely because of the influence of their parents' standard of living, conservative attitude, and quest for perfectionism.

As the river flows, so does time. It runs so fast and so smoothly that you barely even notice that it is passing you by. The ripples we create along the way and the boulders that we manage to maneuver are what determines the direction that river may flow. The children of the mid-twentieth century made their mark, their statement, just as every generation does. Do we think we are special because of it? I don't think so. I believe we lived in a good *place in time* where we lived without borders, without fear, and without inhibitions. It was a fortunate time, but the focus doesn't stay on the past and the living isn't there. The *place in time* is today.

"Respect where you came from and what has been given to you. You are capable of passing on goodness, and the goodness that you give will last into eternity."
—D. L. VanderJagt

Works Cited

Cavaliere, Felix, and Eddie Brigati. People Got To Be Free. The Rascals. The Rascals with Arif Mardin, 1968. Vinyl recording.

Dylan, Bob. My Back Pages. The Byrds. 1967. Vinyl recording.

Dylan, Bob. The Times They Are A-Changin' Bob Dylan. 1963. Vinyl recording.

Harburg, Edgar Y. The Lollipop Guild. The Munchkins in The Wizard of Oz. 1939. Vinyl recording.

Holler, Dick. Abraham, Martin and John. Dion. Phil Gernhard, 1968. Vinyl recording.

Jagger, Mick, and Keith Richards. Mother's Little Helper. The Rolling Stones. Andrew Loog Oldham, 1965. Vinyl recording.

Julien, Michael, David Shapiro and Ivan Mogul. Let's Live For Today. The Grass Roots. P. F. Sloan and Steve Barri, 1967. Vinyl recording.

Kirkman, Terry. Cherish. The Association. Curt Boettcher, 1966. Vinyl recording.

Reynolds, Allen. Five O'Clock World. The Vogues. Nick Cenci and Tony Moon, 1965. Vinyl recording.

Reynolds, Malvina. Little Boxes. Pete Seeger. 1963. Vinyl recording.

Sainte-Marie, Buffy. By Buffy Sainte-Marie. Universal Soldier. 1964. Vinyl recording.

Sebastian, John, and Mark Sebastian. Summer in the City. The Lovin' Spoonful. Erik Jacobsen, 1966. Vinyl recording.

Sloan, P. F. Let Me Be. The Turtles. 1966. Vinyl recording.

Stills, Stephen. For What It's Worth. Buffalo Springfield. 1967. Vinyl recording.

Storball, Donald. Cool Jerk. The Capitols. Ollie McLaughlin, 1966. Vinyl recording.

Townshend, Peter. My Generation. The Who. Shel Talmy, 1965. Vinyl recording.

Acknowledgments

To my mom: You always asked me when my book would be finished, and now you are reading this from your place in heaven. I wish I could sit down, have a cup of tea with you, and talk about the old times.

To my dad: Always my supporter and my encourager. I have depended upon your knowledge and stability throughout my entire life. You will never know how much that means to me. Thank you.

To my husband, Dale: Your unrelenting "cheerleading" to keep this book going until completion was everything I needed to make it happen. I loved that I could talk with you about the book and the era we lived in. You understood where I was coming from and offered great ideas along the way. I thank you for all the hours you unselfishly gave to me. I couldn't have done this without you.

Author's Bio

Deborah VanderJagt grew up in Ann Arbor, Michigan, where the influences of a Midwestern campus town contributed to her childhood memories. She currently lives on the coast of Lake Michigan, where she raised her family, and enjoys the beauty of the water and the woodlands. She has a degree in business and has worked in the financial industry for twenty-seven years. Writing has always been a fun passion and she enjoys sitting on the beach, wherever it may be in the world, with a journal and a pen in hand.

Made in the USA
Middletown, DE
07 February 2017